W9-BNQ-756

Investigating Performance

Design and Outcomes with xAPI

By Janet Laane Effron and Sean Putman

Publisher: MakingBetter
Designer: Jason Early (gruntmonkey LLC.)
Editor: Megan Bowe (MakingBetter)
Copy Editor: Catherine Skeen

ISBN 978-1-48359-629-7

MakingBetter
Narberth, PA
http://makingbetter.us

First Edition

Table of Contents

Introduction

Time to Get Real

You develop a course, sometimes with intense care and attention to detail, sometimes quickly with a suddenly imposed deadline looming over your head. In the end, though, how do you know if the course did its job? If you did your job? And, more to the point, did the end users get what they needed to do well at their jobs?

You take a course; you know how to play the game. (Standardized testing taught you well.) You can scan for the right information, give the correct responses, make a good guess as far as expectations. You know which videos you can safely ignore, using their playing time to answer a few emails. And all will be forgotten in a few hours or days or weeks, except maybe a few vague concepts, a random cartoon, or a point of cognitive dissonance.

You go to conferences and read blog posts where everyone is talking about real learning, contextual learning: the ideal scenarios that are rooted in the realities of how people learn rather than the limitations of your LMS. Heck, you might even be speaking at the conferences and writing the blog posts. You want learning to be like that; you want to do great stuff.

But you can't – at least, not using the measuring stick you currently have. It's not that assessment is a bad thing, but when we are working at scale, the measures we have don't really tell us what we need to know.

The Lie That Is Test Scores
"I am not a number, I am a free man!"

Suppose you just got a passing grade on your last elearning test on software training? Or safety training? What does your test score really tell you? Something about knowledge? Or just memory, or pattern recognition?

If I'm solving a problem or answering a question simply by recognizing the form and recalling the rubrics, that doesn't say much about whether I actually understand what I am doing; it speaks to knowledge more than understanding. (See, for example, Oppenheimer on fluency and priming.)

If we look at learning as a continuum, from Recognition to Recall to Re-creation (or Application, or Creation), the kind of learning that ties to performance is generally in the last category, but the kind of testing available in most elearning is designed primarily to assess the first two, which, for learning professionals, is both limiting and frustrating. Limiting, because it forces us to design to a specific form of assessment, and frustrating, because we know we could give our learners so much more, something so much better, but we need to be able to quantify and validate what we do. We don't usually have the luxury of one-on-one coaching or individual assessment of transfer to performance. And we can never be sure, if test results are poor, or if they are excellent, whether the root cause is the learner, the course, or some proportion of both.

Then there's also the painful reality that testing, as a form of assessment, comes too late in the process. The course has been designed, built, and launched; end users have worked their way through it, and it's only at the end of this enormous investment of time and resources that we attempt to determine if the course did its job.

The Need for Better

We know that all the talk at conferences about the need for real

learning, for meaningful, contextual learning, isn't just aspirational, and that it's not a luxury, it's necessary. Necessary for the organization to have the knowledge, skills and insight to meet it's goals. Necessary for the employees to succeed and advance in their work.
If we want to be effective in what we deliver, it's also necessary to know what aspects of our courses are working long before we're seeing test results. We have all the tools we need to iterate our design and resources except the critical tool: ongoing feedback from end users.

It's become increasingly possible to do better. Barriers to information and data access have dropped dramatically over the past decade, and with a few tools and a good game plan, we're well positioned to use that information to understand how our end users see our courses and how they are learning, really, in both formal and informal ways.

The Opportunity

With the launch of the Experience API (xAPI) we started looking more closely at how to use data not just to evaluate learners, but to evaluate and support every aspect of learning within organizations – from course development, to understanding learning channels outside of courses, to understanding the performance impacts of learning experiences.

When we use data analysis to understand what's working and what's not working in organizational learning, here's the key: Focus more on what the data tells us about how to improve what we're doing, and less on what it tells us about what end users are doing.

In the chapters ahead, we'll be looking at data around all aspects of learning, from course development, to feedback loops, to performance assessment, as well as big-picture questions about approaches that meet organizational needs.

But what about Big Data? Fortunately for learning professionals who are adding data analysis to their professional toolkit, most of what we deal with isn't on the scale of Big Data. We are concerned with "intelligent data" – that is, the right data to answer our questions, inform decisions, and drive improvements. This means we can get started with analysis using tools that are already familiar.

Opportunity for Design Improvements

We'll start with a look at how data collection and analysis can be used to improve not just instructional design but also the user interface design for the course. Data collection and data awareness start in the design phase, during prototyping. We will also talk about assessing what user data should be collected in the context of the course, to ascertain trends about which elements of the course are delivering value, causing confusion, or excluding or being ignored by different user groups. We can also investigate which outside activities we want to include in our data collection.

Opportunity for Meaningful Measures

The overriding question that gets asked about most courses is, "Did it work?" The answer to this question is rarely found in test scores. Through tools such as xAPI, we can dig deeper, investigating what course elements are effective, not just in test results, but in real world results.

We'll be discussing measures of learner performance within the course content and, equally important, performance of the course content to meet learner needs. There's the opportunity to drill deeper and analyze the value of specific course content for different user groups, as well as see where employees are learning outside of the course and how those other experiences and resources have been beneficial. And of course we will look at how to use data to measure learning where it really matters: performance in context.

Analytics

The data we collect is the starting point, and we'll always approach design and data collection with analysis in mind. The focus in analysis is multifaceted; it means looking beyond analyzing user performance to analyzing course performance in both content and design. We can frame analysis, like data collection, to consider both leading and trailing measures of performance, supporting learners better and efficiently iterating and improving courses based on feedback loops.

The tools are in place to support meaningful, actionable assessment of course design and learner achievement. Now it's time to roll up our sleeves and put those tools to work.

Chapter 1

Defining Statement Properties

Before getting into the basics of data manipulation, it is important to understand how data is going to be collected. In this chapter, we are going to talk about the Experience API (xAPI). The Experience API allows activities to be tracked as learners perform them, and this chapter will introduce and define the objects and properties that go into collecting xAPI data. If you are a non-developer (which you might be if you're reading this book) the xAPI specification may seem completely overwhelming. After all, it is intended for developers who are creating software, scripts, or apps that will be generating data. Fortunately, many software vendors have created applications that will generate xAPI data. For example, most of the popular rapid development tools for elearning will generate output in an xAPI format. There are also quite a few open source libraries that are available for use in custom applications. Once integrated into the application, they can do the heavy lifting of making xAPI statements.

What we want to help instructional designers (IDs) and developers understand is, what is available in the output of xAPI? What data is available for analytics when using xAPI? In this chapter we will help unpack the xAPI specification into terms that make sense for IDs.

Basic Term Definitions

First, let's learn some xAPI vocabulary, which will help us understand the statement generation process and all the pieces in the ecosystem that generate and store xAPI statements. Some terms will be defined as we go, but a few basic terms are:

Activity – An action that is being tracked in conjunction with a verb. In terms of a statement, it is something that somebody did. If we look at a simple statement, "Sean wrote a book," "book" is the activity in regards to the xAPI statement. Activities can consist of almost anything real or virtual.

Activity Statement – In its simplest form, the activity statement is made up of an actor, a verb, and an object that are tied back to an activity. The actor states who performed the action. The verb states the action performed. The object is what the action was performed on. The statement can then reference an activity that provides a broader context for the statement. In xAPI, a statement is the method for collecting and storing data as a chunk of JSON.

Application Programming Interface (API) – A defined way for a piece of software to communicate with other software. When an API communicates, the communication is referred to as a "call". Just as you might make a phone call to communicate information, an API makes a call to communicate data.

Learning Record Store (LRS) – The LRS is a system that uses APIs to move and store statements. An LRS must be present for xAPI to function. An LRS is not required by the specification to have any data visualization. It is meant to store statements and related data as will be shown throughout this and subsequent chapters.

Learning Record Provider (LRP) – The learning record provider is the origin of the statement that communicates with the LRS. It might be similar to a SCORM package that has all the learning assets within. It can also be a separate entity, such as a software package, that is separate from the activity.

JavaScript Object Notation (JSON) – JSON is a syntax for storing and exchanging data. It is the data format in which the statements are written. The simple format makes it easy for the data to be passed from LRS to LRS. Below is an example of JSON for a simple statement:

Example statement:

This statement is describing the activity 'Sean Putman *attempted* xAPI Statements.'

```
{
    "version": "1.0.0",
    "actor": {
        "objectType": "Agent",
        "name": "Sean Putman",
        "mbox": "mailto:sputman34@gmail.com"
    },
    "object": {
        "objectType": "Activity",
        "id": "http://learnxapi.com/gb_xapi_content/\test/",
        "definition": {
            "description": {
                "und": ""
            },
            "name": {
                "und": "xAPI Statements"
            },
            "type": "http://adlnet.gov/expapi/activities/course"
        }
    },
    "verb": {
        "id": "http://adlnet.gov/expapi/verbs/attempted"
    },
    "id": "e0c00630-5d50-4c5f-83c9-7c1d5580777d",
    }
```

Usually a LRS will not show the statement in JSON in the default view; it will show it in a human readable form similar to how it's written above the JSON example. The JSON is stored in the database and can be queried for data visualization or other tools.

There are many other terms to become familiar with as the chapter moves along. Understanding the terms above is a good jump start into knowing what goes into a statement and how the properties, or different parts of a statement, can work together. More terms will be defined in context throughout the chapter.

Statement Basics

What goes into a basic statement? Some of the required parts of a statement will be added by the software (e.g. timestamps). From the point of view of an instructional designer there are three main items to consider when making a statement. (To make a statement even better, other properties can be considered, but these will be discussed later.) The main three are: actor, verb and object, or "I did something." Each statement has three requirements:

- Each property (actor, verb, object) cannot be used more than once.
- There must be an actor, a verb, and an object.
- The statement can list these properties (actor, verb, object) in any order.

A fourth property that is recommended is an ID, or identifier, for the statement. The ID property should be set by the learning record provider (software or library), but if for some reason it is not, then the LRS will add one when the statement is stored. In other words, if the LRP does not provide a unique way to identify a statement, the LRS must do this before it can accept the statement because otherwise there will be no way to find the statement again. Most rapid development tools give a unique ID to statements generated from their published outputs. Custom solutions (HTML-based, or Apps) will need to be programmed to create the unique ID. It is recommended that the originating program (the LRP) create the unique ID, especially if other programs will need to use the statement. When the LRS creates an ID, it is known only to the LRS, which makes it a more complicated process to use that particular statement.

Required Statement Properties

To help understand the statement structure and the basic statement, let's start at the beginning with the actor.

Actor

The actor is the person, group, or system who did something. The actor attribute can have a single actor, a group identifying the actors, or a group in which individual actors are not identified. As stated above, a statement requires an actor.

What does an actor need to have? The actor can be one of two objectTypes: an Agent (one individual or system) or a Group (more than one individual). There are certain requirements when identifying the agent and several things to avoid. The agent must use one of the four types of **inverse functional identifiers.**

Whoa. Let's take a step back and define the inverse functional identifier. In simple terms, it is a unique way to identify a person, group, or system, it is just a more technical way to say it. The four unique ways to identify an agent are:

- **mbox** – An email address that has been and will only ever be assigned to this person. In even more basic terms, it means the email address needs to be unique to this person in the past, now, and in the future. It must use a format of "mailto:email address".
- **mbox_sha1sum** – This is essentially an email address, but it uses a mathematical function to hide the email address. This would be used for privacy. This is especially common when a company is using an LRS which is not inside their firewall.
- **openID** – openID is a specification for unique, anonymous identification across web services. It is used across existing sources such as Google, Yahoo, Wordpress, and many others.

- **account** - An account on an existing intranet, LMS, or other system that can be used to identify the agent.

If you are launching a course and modules, the actor identifier will depend greatly on the system that is performing the launch. In some cases, as when using an existing LMS or a launcher, the account used to log in will be the identifier. An mbox will normally be part of the account information, as the statement JSON will show. Below is an example of the statement JSON for the actor that is stored in the LRS from an LMS or launcher as described above:

```
{
"version": "1.0.0",
"actor": {
"objectType": "Agent",
"name": "Sean Putman",
"mbox": "mailto:sputman34@gmail.com"
},
```

If using only the mbox, the name attribute above would not appear in the JSON for the statement.

Agent

An agent has three properties available: objectType, name, and inverse functional identifier (the unique way to identify the actor). Name and objectType are optional, but the unique identifier is required. The name will be populated by the account used to run the learning intervention, if available, or the learner can be prompted to enter a name along with an email if it is defined at run time. Run time in this context means that name and email are defined inside the course after it is launched. It is not drawn from a system, like an LMS, but is entered by the learner as the course is running. The objectType needs to be defined only when the agent is used as an object in the statement. An example might be "Janet taught Sean." In this case Janet is the actor agent and Sean is an agent being used as the object.

Each Agent cannot contain more than one unique identifier. This means the agent should not be identified by an email address *and* an account; it should be one or the other. If account is used, the agent should not include an email address to define an mbox. Furthermore, individuals should not have an identifier that is also used to identify a group of people.

Questions to ask when defining the Agent:

- Is agent the right way to identify the learners using the intervention?
- Can the agent information be obtained from another system?
- What is the unique identifier being used for the agent?

Let's continue on to the next type of Actor that can be used: groups.

Groups

With an objectType of group, a group of people are set as the actor. The group is a collection of agents and can be used in most of the same situations as an individual. There are two types of groups available for use: anonymous and identified.

Anonymous Group

An anonymous group is defined in the specification as "a cluster of people where there is no ready identifier for this cluster." For example, an ad hoc team is created for a project, but there is no obvious and unique way to identify this ad hoc group. To solve the issue, we use the objectType of group and list an identifier for each member of the group. An anonymous group has three available properties, two of which are required. The objectType must be set to "Group," and a property named "member" must contain a list of the group members and a unique identifier for each member. The name property is optional and would contain a name for the group. The anonymous group must not contain an inverse functional identifier (remember it is just a unique way to identify the actor). Each anonymous group will be treated as a unique group, even if the members are the same.

Identified Group

This type has a unique identifier that is used to identify the group. There are four properties associated with it: objectType (which is set to "Group"); name; member; and a unique identifier. The name property is optional. The name could be used in analytics as a way to identify and filter for the group. The member property is also optional because the unique identifier for the group is mandatory. Since the group is identified and has a unique identifier, we have other methods of determining the group members. Obviously, the unique identifier is necessary to uniquely identify the group, but a unique identifier for each of the individuals in the group is optional. Since the group has a unique identifier, we do not need a unique identifier for each individual member. Remember, an individual cannot also use the group identifier. The identifier is not unique if both a group and an individual can use it.

Questions to ask when defining a Group:

- Is the group the right way to identify the learners using the intervention?
- What type of group is this, anonymous or identified?
- Is there a name for the group?
- Should I add identifiers for the individuals in the group?

Conclusion

We have many options for identifying the Actor for the statements. Often the Actor will be an individual identified by an account through an LMS or some other means. We should remain aware that the Actor is flexible and provides options for tracking similar groups of people with statements. With the Actor set, it is time to move to the second piece of the statement; the Verb.

Verb

As the specification states, "the Verb defines the action between Actor and Activity." This means that the verb describes the action performed by the Actor on something. The specification itself does not specify verbs. However, an ADL registry identifies verbs and prescribes definitions so that verbs consistent in usage and definition across the community, regardless of the use case. The verbs have a consistent IRI which means they can be referenced by the statements generated.

Verbs have two properties assigned to them. The ID property is required and the display property is not required, but recommended. The ID is commonly referred to as the IRI (Internationalized Resource Identifier) of the Verb. It is simply a Verb definition. The IRI is human readable and contains the meaning of the Verb. The display makes the statement human readable. The display property cannot change the meaning of the verb. Here is an example of a statement showing the verb with no display property set and one with the display set. The IRI is a URL to a simple web page that shows the definition, the display property and potentially other language displays of the verb. Here is an example of an IRI page. Any system that reads the verb uses the IRI to define the meaning. You can see the IRI information stored with the statement here in the JSON:

No display property:

```
"version": "1.0.0",
  "id": "a004beef-ed90-48d3-85e3-d40c6748c8ef",
  "timestamp": "2016-05-23T14:09:40.322Z",
  "actor": {
    "objectType": "Agent",
    "mbox": "mailto:sputman34@gmail.com",
    "name": "Sean Putman"
  },
  "verb": {
    "id": "http://www.learnxapi.com/clicked.htm"
  },
```

Display property:

```
"version": "1.0.0",
  "id": "3d1f3a0d-159e-4370-aaa5-2e46173b3eb6",
  "timestamp": "2016-12-15T19:43:21.177Z",
  "actor": {
    "objectType": "Agent",
    "mbox": "mailto:sputman34@gmail.com",
    "name": "Sean Putman"
  },
  "verb": {
    "id": "http://adlnet.gov/expapi/verbs/attempted",
    "display": {
      "und": "attempted"
    }
  },
  IRI Page:
    "id": "http://adlnet.gov/expapi/verbs/attempted",
    "display": {
      "und": "attempted"
    }
  },
```

IRI Page:

Property	Description	Type
id	http://www.⬛⬛⬛⬛⬛/clicked.htm	id
name	{"en-US" : "clicked"}	Language Map
display	{"en-US" : "clicked"}	Langauge Map
description	{"en-US" : "A verb specifying that the user has clicked somethig ont eh web page.	Language Map

The IRI must identify which meaning the verb is representing. The display property usually will display the verb in the past tense. In the examples before, it is "fired" not fire or fires. However if it makes sense to use another tense of the verb for an activity, we have the flexibility to do so. The Verb is not tied to any specific language. The IRI simply defines the meaning of the verb regardless of language.

Verbs and Activities

The specification describes the creation process so that "communities of practice" can establish Verbs. A community of practice is a group of people who share a profession and/or a craft. In the case of xAPI the communities of practice can get together and decide on a language that will be used for statements generated by the community. They can decide which verbs will best meet the needs of the statements generated by the that community. xAPI communities of practice also generate profiles, lists, and repositories around the vocabulary. Already, the ADL has put together communities of practice for xAPI, listed at https://www. adlnet.gov/adl-collaboration/xapi-community-of-practice/.

When a community of practice sets up verbs, the new Verb must own the IRI or have owner permission to be used to denote an xAPI verb. A new verb should have a human readable description with the verb's intended usage. Creating a usage description for the verb informs other people of its meaning and how it should be used. When we work through Verbs and decide on the vocabulary, it is important to use existing verbs whenever possible. This enables a common language to be used across communities of practice, potentially making cross-community analytics easier to perform. Using existing verbs also allows for commonality for future projects. When we use a consistent existing verb we enable everyone to start from a consistent platform.

If no suitable verb exists, we can create a new verb. We should be judicious about creating new verbs, however, to avoid data collisions. For example, we can imagine a company wanting to define a vocabulary entirely unto themselves using language that reflects their corporate culture. In such a scenario, the off-the-shelf tools that use established vocabularies would create statements that would go unused. This is why new verbs should be confirmed with a community of practice, to set the vocabulary that community needs. The resulting vocabulary will be the language used consistently by the entire community when talking about an activity. With commonality, we can ensure data portability if statements need to be moved. When vocabularies differ, statements moved from one entity to another will not match, even if they talk about the same activity.

The new verb should have a valid IRI. Here is an example of a custom verb:

Property	Description	Type
id	▓▓▓▓▓▓▓▓▓▓▓▓▓▓▓▓▓▓▓▓▓▓/verbs/created.htm	id
name	{"en-US" : "created"}	Language Map
display	{"en-US" : "created"}	Langauge Map
description	{"en-US" : "A verb specifying that the user has created an entity from within a panel	Language Map

A community of practice can share its list of verbs with anyone, for use when performing defined actions. The members of the community (which could include individuals, companies, and industry organizations) decide which verbs are meaningful for that community. The specification is not the right place for the list, because, the limited definition would hinder the capture of all experiences. For example the verb "fired" might mean "shot something". This narrow definition limits other opportunities to use the verb "fired". A statement might appear as "John fired the cannon," but in a different context, such as terminating employment, the same verb has a different meaning. If the specification had prescribed the meaning of the verb "fired", the community of practice would not have the ability to set the meaning of the verb.

The community of practice can pair verbs and activities. A community of practice for human resources might specify employment as an activity. One verb that might relate to the activity of employment is "terminated". In this case terminate means to end an action when tied to employment. A community of practice for electrical engineers might use terminate, but paired with the activity of running a circuit. Different contexts tie verbs to different activities. Communities need to pair verbs with activities in order to complete their meaning and give them context for that community. Doing so differentiates the combination so that the statements themselves have context. This allows us to categorize and analyze the data in a more efficient manner. If we categorize by "terminated" only, we get a list of both use cases. If we have the activity, then we categorize into "terminated" and the two activities in which it is used. Now I have a more granular data set to use.

Questions to ask when deciding on the Verb:

- Is there an existing verb in the registry that I can use?
- If there is an existing verb, is the context correct for my usage?
- Is there a community of practice for my industry?
- If I need to create a verb, is there an existing template with a community of practice to create the verb?
- If no community of practice, is there an industry group that can help set the vocabulary?

Object

Objects can be almost anything, including an activity, an agent, a group, a sub-statement, or a statement reference. Here are examples of each type:

Activity as Object: "Sean completed an application."
Agent as Object: "Janet interviewed Sean."
Sub-Statement as Object: "Janet responded to 'Sean completed an application'."

The final example in the list can also apply to a statement reference, which means that the statement being generated refers to another statement as the object. While the implementation by the learning record provider might be different, the human readable form would look the same. Each of these objects should include an object type property for the statement. If an object type is not specified, the object type will default to Activity.

Object Type is Activity

The object type of activity has a simple set of properties that need to be assigned to it. A unique identifier (IRI) is required for each activity. Further, the unique identifier must always point to the same activity. If two activities were to contain the same identifier, the statements would not necessarily be valid. The LRS is not able to treat two activities as having the same ID. The LRS will treat activities with the same ID as one activity, because it is not capable of deciding that two activities have the same ID. If data from another system is introduced, the LRS cannot tell what is supposed to take place with regard to activities with the same ID. The ID should be created with a scheme ensuring that each ID is unique. The activity ID can point to metadata or link to a document for further definition. The section on definition goes into more detail about using metadata for further definition. The moreInfo property gives more information on linking to external documents.

A definition is optional for each activity. The definition could come from metadata out of another system in JSON format. The LRS can take the JSON data and incorporate it into its definition for the activity. The LRS can make decisions about differing activity definition properties if the learning record provider has the permissions to change the definition. The stored definition can change if the provider has the authority to do so. So if a learning record provider (statement generator) has permissions on the LRS to change the definition property, it can. The LRS can also accept small corrections to the definition, as in the case of a spelling mistake.

Recommended Properties

There are optional properties, but a few of these are recommended. For example, it is recommended to set a name property. This is a readable name for the activity, to be displayed in the statement. During analysis the name provides a way to query and sort the data.

Another recommendation is to set a description for the activity. The description appears in the JSON of the statement and provides further context for the activity. A unique identifier is also recommended for the activity in the type property. The type property will set the type of activity for future statements. As with verbs, we look for existing and established activity types when defining them for consistency.

An optional property for the statement is the moreInfo property. The moreInfo property is a link to a document with information about an activity. The moreInfo property can include a way to launch the activity. Most of the time, moreInfo is simply a link to a document. It is a URL that can be found and used to help define the activity.

Lastly, for activities we can define structures for interactions or assessments. For xAPI those interactions are borrowed from the SCORM 2004, 4th Edition data model. The definitions are simple to use, though limited. They are meant to provide a familiar way to record the interaction data. However, communities of practice that need a better set of interactions can use the extensions property in xAPI (discussed later in this chapter). The interaction activities will contain three properties: interactionType, correctResponsepattern, and a set of interaction components. The interaction type will be set from the SCORM 2004 set of data models. The correct response pattern property defines the correct response for the activity. The interaction components are specific to an interaction type. They include the choices for the activity, the scale, the source of the activity, the target of the activity, or the steps to complete the activity. An ID is required to set the interaction components as defined in the SCORM 2004 specification. We can set a description that tells something about the interaction component, such as the text for an answer in a multiple choice interaction. If there is an array of components for the interaction, each must have a unique ID.

Agent or Group As Object

A person or group can be specified as the object in a statement. The objectype property must be defined as agent or group for this to be valid. The rules regarding an agent being specified as the object follow those for specifying an agent or group as an Actor. The properties specifying the agent or group will be shown in the statement output in the object field as shown in the example:

Statement as Object

A statement can be an object in two scenarios: a Statement reference and a Sub-Statement. The common use case for a Statement reference is grading or commenting on an experience that can be tracked as its own statement. The example above used this statement: Janet responded to 'Sean completed an application'. "Sean completed an application" is a statement on its own. It would be sent to the LRS to document an event. The new statement is stating that Janet commented on the event of Sean completing the application. The statement used for the object is referenced by its ID in the LRS. A statement reference can also be used to comment on an existing statement. In this case, a result would be used to add a comment that references an existing statement ID. The JSON for the statement would appear as follows:

Sub-Statement as Object

A sub-statement is a new statement that cannot stand on its own in the LRS. In the specification for the sub-statement the main use case is identifying something that will happen in the future. An example statement might be, "Megan planned "Megan will visit Up to all of Us location"." The parent statement is using "Megan will visit Up to All of Us location" as the object. The action of visiting the location has not happened yet. Down the road, a statement of "Megan visited Up to All of Us location" will be generated when the activity takes place. The parent statement tells us simply that the future activity has been planned.

Questions to ask when defining the Object:

- What type of object will I need?
- Do I need to refer to another statement with the object?
- Does the object relate to an activity type?
- Is there a consistent vocabulary that needs to be defined for the object?

Additional Statement Properties

The following fields are all optional. As we noted in the beginning of the chapter, the only required fields are an actor, a verb, and an object. The following fields, however, can add more information to the statement. The additional information then adds value during analytics by giving more ways to group, cut, and analyze the data. We also gain additional information as to what took place in an activity. For example, if a statement has the actor, verb object, "Sam passed the test", we have a valid statement, and we know that Sam passed the test. Additional information, such as "Sam passed the test with a score of 95" gives additional information to the statement. Combinations of additional fields provide layers of detail about the activity that is taking place.

Result

The Result object offers a measured outcome to the statement in which it resides. It represents the graded activity outcome for the actor. We can find the Result object in several ways. One way to measure is using a score. The score property is a graded activity of the actor, and the score can be represented in one of four ways. The recommended method is scaled such that a decimal between -1 and 1 represents a percentage. Scaled is used in SCORM 2004 as a method of representing the score. Here is an example of the JSON for a statement with the score set as a scaled value:

The other methods of representing the score can be a raw score, which is a decimal number that can be between a minimum and maximum. The minimum and maximum do not have to be defined in this property. The other two are the min and max. The min is represented as a decimal number less than the max. The max is represented as a decimal number greater than the minimum. The most common method of representing the score property is the scaled number.

Another type of Result object representation is the success property. Success simply indicates whether an attempt on the activity was successful. The statement shows success as a pass or fail. An example statement might read, "Sean answered question correctly." Understanding that the answer was correct is done using the success property, which gives a value of true if the correct answer is given or false if the correct answer is not given. It can also give a score, which will be represented in the statement. The combination of properties says the answer is correct, resulting in a certain value for the score. The success property can also be used in conjunction with a score to signify passing or failing. A failure to reach a score that is set as passing will result in the success property being set to fail. The statement would then read "Sean failed the quiz." The success property would be set to fail for the statement and stored in the LRS.

Next is completion, which acts like the success property. A value of true is given if the activity is completed, and a value of false is given if the activity is still incomplete. We might see this in a statement for a course or module indicating whether it was completed or left incomplete. Depending on the learning record provider, a statement for incomplete might not be generated. Instead, an activity would be assumed incomplete if no statement with the verb completed is generated.

Response is a property used typically with quiz questions or some type of interaction that requires a user input. If used in a question, the response property will hold the answer of the response and, depending on the learning record provider, will append it to the statement. It can work in conjunction with the score and success properties to convey whether an answer is correct.

Duration is a property that tells the period of time in which the statement occurred. It has a precision of 0.01 seconds so it will be very accurate as to the amount of time the activity took.

Finally, extensions can be added to the results object. (More about extensions later.)

Questions to ask when defining the Result:

- What constitutes success?
- What format will the result take?

- Do I need to track a response for each question or is the overall result enough?
- Is duration important to the result?
- Is a pass or fail necessary?

Context

Context is an object that allows additional contextual information to be added to the statement. Context adds more detail as to how the statement might relate to other activities or instructors, or whether it was a team activity.

Context has the ability to link the statement to a registration. The registration can be linked to an attempt of an activity, a session, or a string of activities. A registration can span actors representing a particular activity. Completion of a particular activity does not have to end the registration. The registration can span multiple activities as necessary.

The instructor property can link the statement to an instructor or group of instructors, if not the actor for the statement. In the analytics the instructor can then be used a grouping mechanism for a set of statements.

Like the instructor property, a team property is available to link the statement to a team not specified as the actor. This would allow the statement to be used to track activities related to a team and to be queried in the analytics.

A map of the types of learning activities can be added to the statement. The Contextactivities property allows the statement to be related to other activities through context. Many statements tie into larger activities and do not stand alone, so they need to be related in some sort of structure. Context can be used to relate them in one of four ways: parent, grouping, category, and other. Parent is a direct link between the activity and the object in the statement. For example, a quiz question would have the quiz as a parent. In most cases there would be only one parent activity.

Grouping is an indirect relationship with the activity. An example of this would be a group of courses that make up a certification. The course would relate to the certification in a grouping. We would use the category property to categorize the statement by activity. We use the category to tag the statement with a profile of behaviors. Finally, "other" is a property, a catch-all for items that do not fit in the other categories. A statement might be "Sean creates a spreadsheet for monthly numbers". The spreadsheet refers to the activity, with the monthly numbers being the context in the other property. Values entered here should not cover all the relationships that an object might have. A quiz question might be used across multiple quizzes, but every instance would not be shown in a statement. The statement would directly relate to one parent, not all possible uses of the question. To be clear about which version of an activity is being used, we can use the revision property. The revision property is an open property that allows the revision to be included within the constructs of the statement. The platform property allows us to add a platform. It will define the platform used in the activity. Language is defined in the language property if appropriate for the activity. It is the language in which the activity occurred. A reference to another statement can be added in the statement property. We could use the other statement as context for the activity taking place in the statement. Finally, there is an extensions property available to serve as a place for other items that do not fit in the other properties. Extensions will be discussed later.

Questions to ask when defining the Context:

- Do I need to relate this statement to other activities?
- Is there an instructor for this intervention?
- Do I need to relate this intervention to a larger group?

Timestamp vs Stored

Timestamp means when an activity occurred. The timestamp does not represent when it is stored in the LRS, but when the activity took place. The Stored object is the time when the statement was stored in the LRS. It is key to differentiate this as xAPI allows for offline storage, or there could be network latency in the storage of the statement. The timestamp can represent any point in time over the duration of the activity. Communities of practice should define the right time to record the timestamp for a particular activity. The timestamp and stored objects should include the time zone. A timestamp can also be a moment in the future. A future timestamp would define a deadline for planned learning to take place.

Questions to ask for the Timestamp or Stored date:

- Will I be storing statements offline?
- Is the stored time important to my analytics?
- Do I have deadlines for when an intervention needs to be taken?

Version

The version in this context is the xAPI specification version that the statements follow. The version is important because it makes sure the data can be transferred between LRSs. We find that most learning record providers today are working against the 1.0 specifications. However, if older versions of a learning record provider are being used, then an older version, such as 0.95, might be used to generate the statements. An LRS must accept valid statements with a version starting with 1.0.

Questions to ask for the Version:

- Is my Learning Record Provider using the latest specification?

Attachments

If necessary, attachments can be used as a supplemental piece of information to a statement. There are several use cases for an attachment to a statement. One would be an image of a badge or certificate that would be the result of an activity or set of activities. Or videos, written material, or communications might be stored with a statement. There are several required properties that must be defined for an attachment. First is the usageType property, which is used to define the usage of the attachment. It is a URL that is very similar to the ID for the verb. It is a small html file that describes what the attachment does. The display property is set to display a name for the attachment. The contentType property defines what type of content is found in the attachment – a certain type of image (.png, .jpg, .gif) or whether it is an ascii text file. The length property is required and shows the length of the file in octets. Octets are bytes that show the size of the file. Finally, the sha2 property contains a unique identifier for the attachment. It is recommended that the key be set to a minimum of 256 characters. It is helpful to fill in the optional description property, to give a description of the attachment. If the file resides on a web server, the fileURL property can be filled in with the URL needed to retrieve the file. (This is an optional property as not all files will reside on a web server.)

Questions to ask when defining Attachments:

- Do I need to provide more information for the statement that is generated?
- Where will I store the attachments?
- Is the storage location common for others in the organization?

Retrieval of Statements

Collections of statements can be retrieved from an LRS by performing a query. The retrieval is what will be important when performing analytics on the statements. The statements can be retrieved in a number of ways. Depending on the needs of your analytics you can do this in a manner as simple as a CSV output for use in Excel, or a complex query of the database in the LRS.

Questions to ask for Retrieval of Statements:

- What format does my analytics tool import?
- Can I access the database directly?

- What queries will I need to run to extract the information I need?

Voided Statements

Statements cannot be changed or deleted once they have entered the LRS. If we are moving statements across endpoints, it is critical to make sure that statements are not deleted. Of course, some statements might not be valid indefinitely once they have been stored. If we need to make a statement void because of a mistake, expiration, or other factor, then this is "voiding the statement". The verb "void" has been reserved for issuing a statement that will void another statement. A statement that has been used to void another statement can never be voided. The object of the voiding statement will use a StatementRef and the statement ID to identify the statement being voided. If a voided statement needs to be added back, the learning record provider should create a new statement with a new ID for the activity.

Questions to ask when Voiding statements:

- Do I need to set an expiration on a statement? (i.e. certification renewal)

Signed Statements

A statement may include a digital signature to provide authenticity and integrity to the statement. A statement might need a signature if there is regulatory or legal significance to the statement. Signatures are used if the learning record provider is not a valid source of authorization. Signatures also allow third party systems to validate statements. The signature is an attachment to the statement to which it is applied.

Questions to ask for Signed Statements:

- Is there an authorization required for the statement to give it authenticity?

- What third party validator do I need to sign the statements?
- Is my learning record provider adequate for providing authorization?

Most of the items defined in this chapter are optional for an xAPI statement, and yet in some combination they will prove critical to perform meaningful analytics on the statements saved in an LRS. If you are not going to be building applications and libraries from scratch, then the statements provided by the learning record provider will limit you. Not all learning record providers provide the option to decide what is included in the statement. You will have more flexibility when using an open source library and coding how your content interacts with the library. The library does the heavy lifting, while you link your content to generate some of these additional fields.

From this chapter you can take away a working knowledge of what is available in an xAPI statement, giving you the background to talk to developers if necessary, or to understand what is available when you start to query and group data. Building something from scratch requires a deeper understanding of the specification than has been provided here.

You now understand the basic (and a bit more) xAPI statement. Building statements is the "easy" part of starting out with xAPI. The tricky part is figuring out how you want to structure the data and how you want to use the data. In the next chapter we look at how to use vocabulary and profiles to make statements that are consistent in language and structure. Creating statements in this way will greatly improve the data output when it is time to run some analytics.

References

Bowe, Megan. 2013. "It's Time For Profiles – Tin Can API". *Tincanapi.Com*. http://tincanapi.com/its-time-for-profiles/.

"Overview – Tin Can API". 2014. *Tincanapi. Com*. http://tincanapi.com/overview/.

"Sharing Statements Between Courses – Tin Can API". 2014. *Tincanapi.Com*. http://tincanapi. com/share-statements-between-courses/.

"Statements 101 – Tin Can API". 2014. *Tincanapi.Com*. https://tincanapi.com/statements-101/#verbsvsactivities.

Chapter 2

xAPI Vocabulary and Profiles

Thinking about designing and collecting with xAPI can be overwhelming. Almost anything can be tracked in any number of different ways with xAPI as the method to collect data. Many verbs can have multiple meanings, which can muddy the waters of data analysis. How, as a community of practitioners, do we address this? The basic requirement for xAPI data is only that it be written in JSON format so that information can be passed among multiple systems. The specification does not address how the statements are structured in terms of vocabulary and wording. Anyone using xAPI can potentially define and use their own interpretation of a set of verbs. For this reason, the ADL has written a companion to the xAPI specification to address vocabularies. It is the first attempt as a community to define guidelines for creating and publishing vocabularies. This companion document promotes best practices for semantic definitions of new verbs and vocabularies.

In this chapter we explain why vocabularies and consistent verb usage allow us to make the most effective use of xAPI. We also define and describe "profiles," a term with its own meaning in the xAPI context. In short, profiles help the community define consistent use cases for vocabulary and statement creation.

Vocabulary (Verbs and Activity Types)

The more we think about xAPI data analysis, the better we appreciate the importance of defining and using verbs and activity types consistently, because verbs and activity types play such a large role in categorizing the data that is going to be analyzed. Activity types, like verbs, allow a further categorization: placing statements with the same activity type together. Some existing activity types include: courses, assessments, and simulations. If we want robust analytics, then we need commonality between the verbs and activity types that are used to construct the statements.

To ensure consistent usage, we should construct a data model for the verbs and activity types. A data model standardizes and organizes the data elements and their relation to each other. In the case of xAPI, we would see the links between the verb and its definition in the context in which it is being used. In addition, we can use the activity type to help define the context in which the verb is being used. In the JSON of each statement, the verb ID and the activity ID contain an IRI that defines each. If we define this relationship then we can ensure that the definition is consistent across the statements using that verb and activity type. If we do not use consistent vocabulary, then the data will need considerable work to be useful.

Let's look at an example based on a simple course (an activity type) completion. If one instructional designer uses "completed" as the verb to show a course completion we get a statement like: Learner completed Course 1. If the same learner takes a course created by an instructional designer who uses the verb "finished" to show course completion, we get a statement like: Learner finished Course 2.

Will it be easy to correlate the data for what the learner has completed? Somehow we will have to relate "completed" to "finished" to get a record of what the learner has done in these courses. However if we want to use the two verbs, we can use activity type as a way to categorize them. For "completed" we could use an activity type of course to identify it. For the verb "finished" we could use an activity type of assessment. Our data model could then specify that "finished" is related to assessments, while "completed" is related to courses. This is a fairly simple example; when we get into interactions, the waters can get muddier.

Another way to map the verbs to each other is through data modeling. A data model is a conceptual map of how items relate to one another, which in this case would be verbs and activity types. For example, if we want to tie a number of verbs to a completion, we can set up a data model to show how the verbs work together to form a completed task. A data model can be used to map activity types, such as how a group of modules work together to make up a course. The data model can then be shared with the rest of the department, company, maybe even the industry.

A shared meaning for an entire industry drives standards that can be shared across companies. Communities of practice are cropping up because of this common need. In a community of practice, groups of people get together and define a common practice for using vocabulary (among other items) which will then be a constant for the industry. When practices are defined, creating a common vocabulary set, analytics improve. Further, vendors and tool manufacturers can potentially use this information to build the vocabulary directly into tools. Consistent vocabulary also makes the translation of verbs into other languages much easier as the usage will be defined and constrained, with no guessing about the use of a certain verb and activity type.

What if the same verb has multiple meanings? A defined vocabulary can help solve that problem, too. In the xAPI specification the example verb might be "fired". Statements could be: "John fired a gun." "John fired Joe from his job." The IRI for the verb will give the definition that is being used in this particular use case. A data model can help identify these verbs for a community of practice that, in turn, will define for the industry how the verbs will be used and in what context they will be used. Context is important when we start to look at semantic technologies that will extend the capabilities of xAPI. Based on context, we can tell people where to go next, how to improve themselves, or what others in their position have used to improve themselves.

The ADL Companion specification helps define the structure in which the vocabulary is defined. It uses semantic web structures to define how developers should set up the vocabulary that a tool uses. Many industries and applications use semantic webs to structure data modeling, data sharing, data reuse, and the use of data from many sources in analytics.

A key structure is the RDF (Resource Description Framework) data structure. The RDF data structure uses IRIs to support a global identifier for things or concepts. Key to the thinking behind the xAPI specification is the ability to map to vocabulary IRIs, which gives meaning and metadata, associated to the vocabulary. Part of what RDF does is link unstructured information to semantic meaning and structure. The link helps with translation and labeling of the related information. When information is linked to a structure, we have better ways of sharing and understanding the information. In some cases the information being linked is stuff that cannot be transferred electronically. A concept, for example, is a type of information. Verbs and activity types are considered abstract concepts. Concepts can be documented using many different types of items, such as definitions and different types of notes. Concepts can also have different labels, with a preferred label defined for each language. When designing a dataset for vocabulary, authors have many options for designing the IRIs and their location. Authors should keep in mind the importance of supporting human-readable and machine-readable documents for the dataset(s). It is important to make sure the IRIs are going to be stable for the future. If an IRI is defined, and then lost for any reason, also lost would be the correct definition, the usage, and the date last updated, among other information. The community needs a strategy to ensure that IRIs are persistent (able to be reached). Thus the Companion Vocabulary specification helps address some of these issues.

Currently, the ADL supports requests to create new IRIs. The high level process for defining a new IRI is as follows:

1. Verify that the term does not already exist.
2. The new dataset must follow the design practices outlined in the Companion Specification.
3. Generate and publish the IRI using the classes and properties in the specification.
4. Use the services defined in the specification to create and maintain the new IRI.

At its basic level, xAPI vocabulary can be set up as a linked dataset. A linked dataset is a way to share common meaning and identifiers across the community. This makes vocabulary terms for verbs and activity types available in a reliable and consistent list for use by the community. An example of a linked dataset is the cmi5 verb set that has been identified. (See the sidebar for more information on the cmi5 verb dataset.)

Sidebar
cmi5

According to Art Werkenthin, the cmi5 profile is using xAPI as a way to obtain xAPI data with the LMS launching content. What cmi5 provides is a prescribed set of verbs to make the actions performed consistent in vocabulary. While xAPI on its own provides an open set of verbs, cmi5 provides a set of verbs with consistent definitions. The verbs and definitions defined in the cmi5 specification are as follows:

- **Launched** – A "Launched" statement indicates that the LMS has launched the Assignable Unit (AU). It should be used in combination with the "Initialized" statement sent by the AU in a reasonable period of time to determine whether the AU was successfully launched.
- **Initialized** – The AU uses an "Initialized" statement to indicate that it has been fully started and is ready for student interaction. It must follow the "Launched" statement created by the LMS within a reasonable period of time.
- **Completed** – The AU records the "Completed" statement when the learner has experienced all relevant material in the AU.
- **Passed** – The AU issues the "Passed" statement when the learner has attempted and successfully passed the judged activity in the AU.
- **Failed** – The AU records a "Failed" statement

when the learner has attempted and failed the judged activity in the AU.

- **Abandoned** – The LMS uses the "Terminated" statement to determine that the AU session has ended. In the absence of a "Terminated" statement the LMS will determine whether an AU abnormally terminated a session by monitoring new statements or State API calls made for the same learner/course registration for a different AU. When abnormal termination is detected, the LMS writes an "Abandoned" statement.
- **Waived** – A "Waived" statement is used by the LMS to indicate that the AU may be skipped by the Learner. The LMS makes this determination based on the course structure in cmi5.
- **Terminated** – The AU must record a statement containing the "Terminated" verb as the last statement recorded by the AU in a session.
- **Satisfied** – The LMS writes a "Satisfied" statement when the learner has met the "move on" criteria for all AUs in a block or all AUs in a course.

These prescribed verbs are used consistently for the actions described, giving us defined actions. By using the consistent verb set, this list of verbs makes the content interoperable. These verbs must be used as specified, but cmi5 also makes it possible to use additional verbs as needed as long as they do not clash with the defined verb set. These additional statements are recorded by the LRS just as they would in an xAPI implementation.

It is not necessary for all users of xAPI to create their own vocabulary. Communities of practice are at work, defining vocabulary sets and profiles for creating statements, and we can find links to communities of practice on the ADL website. The communities look at profiles and vocabularies to use existing options whenever practical for the community. Reusing verbs listed by ADL ensures that IRIs will be persistent and that the vocabulary usage is consistent. If a community of practice does not exist for an organization or industry, it is good practice to use the vocabulary that the industry uses. Professional organizations, such as AIA (American Institute for Architects) or SAE (Society of Automotive Engineers), can be a good resource to define the vocabulary used by the industry. If we use industry language as a starting point, then the statements will make sense for the industry and be consistent with the actual work and activities that take place.

Sidebar
Medbiquitous Community of Practice

One example of a community of practice is the working group at MedBiquitous that is developing xAPI profiles for the medical community. Their website states:
"The mission of the MedBiquitous Learning Experience Working Group is to develop a set of xAPI profiles to provide guidance around specific types of activities, including the following:

- Simulations (Virtual patients, Mannekin-based simulations, Preceptor-reviewed simulations, Virtual worlds/games, Standardized patients, etc)
- Clinical Training activities/experiences

In addition to profiles, the working group may create verbs for use within the profiles. Verbs may be applicable across multiple profiles."

Therefore, this working group is setting the vocabulary and setting definitions for the profile or profiles that are needed for the medical community. So far the group has identified seven profiles for training the medical community. The profiles contain instructions for creating statements, which define verb usage and activities for the profile. They have set up a template for creating verbs (if verb creation is necessary) to ensure commonality in the verb definition. They also encourage finding existing verbs before creating a new one, and the working group's website includes a list of defined verbs. The listed verbs contain the definition and the IRI as they pertain to the community.

Another key tool for data interoperability is the profile. What is the profile, and how is it used to prescribe rules for statement generation?

Profiles

Profiles are a way to describe how a certain type of learning or performance activity will be documented by statements. Profiles contain several things to help define statements: they give the structure, required objects, required properties, and object identifiers. Profiles ensure that common activities are consistent between developers and communities of practice. Profiles can reference the items contained within the vocabulary such as verbs, activity types, any extensions used, and any specified usage of attachments.

Let's look at an example of what a profile might contain:

- **Activity types** – Profiles list specific activities from which we can choose an activity. Rules prescribe when to use each activity and its correct usage.
- **Properties that apply to all of the statements** – The profile will prescribe the properties that are required for all statements generated by the profile. It will also prescribe any optional fields for the profile.
- **Time** – If time needs to be tracked for an activity, the profile should describe how the time will be tracked.
- **Workflow** – Does a certain set of statements make up a completed activity? If so, then the profile sets the order and number of statements.

A profile can also have a set of requirements and rules for using xAPI in a particular context. There are generally two types profiles: project and activity profiles. An example of a project profile would be CMI-5. Project profiles meet a higher level need by providing overall profile definitions. As stated above, for example, cmi 5 gives a defined set of verbs that will be used consistently. In addition to the verbs, it gives specific mechanisms for launching content, authentication, managing sessions, creating a reporting structure, and specific rules around course structures. These definitions provide the mechanisms for consistent usage and implementation of cmi5. Activity Profiles can then be created for the more granular activities that need to be defined. An activity profile might be created for the more granular activities of things like assessments or simulations. The profile creates the standards for using the activities in a consistent manner, potentially inside a larger project profile.

Profiles provide a vocabulary of terms; some terms might be created just for this profile and some might be taken from other vocabularies. A profile is not necessary and is not always created, but it is useful as a way to group multiple vocabularies that are situation-dependent and provide consistency to statement generation.

All of the elements described above are used by developers and communities of practice as ways to define the creation and make-up of statements in a consistent manner. We find that the consistency of statements generated is critical when analyzing the data collected. It bears repeating, over and over: consistency in collected data means less cleanup of data for analytics. It also allows the data to be shared between systems in a particular industry or community as the vocabulary and statement make-up will be consistent.

References

Bowe, Megan. 2014. "Delivering On The Experience API – Makingbetter." *Makingbetter.* http://makingbetter.us/2014/01/delivering-on-the-experience-api/.

Miller, Brian. 2014. "Crafting Statements: Choosing the Right Verb (Get to the Point) – Tin Can API." *Tincanapi.Com.* http://tincanapi.com/crafting-statements-choosing-right-verb-get-point/.

Werkenthin, Art. 2016. "Experience API, Cmi5, And Future SCORM." *Learning Solutions Magazine.* http://www.learningsolutionsmag.com/articles/1697/experience-api-cmi5-and-future-scorm/pageall.

Wiggins, Craig, Peter Berking, and Steve Foreman. 2014. "Ten Steps To Plan & Communicate Your xAPI Design to a Web Developer." *Learning Solutions Magazine.* http://www.learningsolutionsmag.com/articles/1523/ten-steps-to-plan--communicate-your-xapi-design-to-a-web-developer#.VDwcXCUQusc.twitter

2016."AICC/CMI-5_Spec_Current." *Github.* https://github.com/AICC/CMI-5_Spec_Current/blob/quartz/cmi5_spec.md#verbs.

Chapter 3

Let the Data Guide You

Introduction to Qualitative and Quantitative Data

Data is abundant and useful. It's also messy, and difficult to use well.

You can pull data from a spreadsheet, an Enterprise Resource Planning system (ERP), a Learning Management System (LMS) and/or activity statements made using the Experience API (xAPI). Wherever you're getting data from, it's good odds that you're collecting it for a reason. You have questions to answer, decisions to make, future goals to evaluate, and experiments to perform. Data is an essential raw material, and it has a tale to tell.

When we start digging into data and its analysis, it's helpful to keep in mind that we're not simply telling a story with data, we are finding the stories locked within the data. While it's natural to go into data analysis with goals, and it's easy to look for the answers we want or expect to find, the truth is that the most useful and interesting information emerges when we let the data guide our exploration.

The 2015 Volkswagen emissions cheating scandal is an extreme example of the kind of information, the kind of story, that is discovered only when you explore data intelligently. Two professors and two graduate students from West Virginia University received a grant to study the emissions of clean diesel vehicles. When the data rolled in, the researchers noticed inconsistencies between standard emission test data and real-world performance. After ruling out errors in their modeling and testing methodology, they dug deeper and found the root cause. By following their data and exploring unexpected results, they went from being obscure academic researchers to front-page news.

While most of us won't ever break open a global scandal with our data analysis, understanding how data works and how to analyze it well is the key to moving beyond simple reporting into actionable insights or meaningful assessments. The first step to good analysis is to consider the nature of data.

Quantitative and Qualitative Data

When we think of data, we typically think of numbers. Height and weight, miles-per-gallon, ticket resolution time, test scores, time-to-completion. Big Data sounds like the Matrix, like a stream of endless numbers. Numbers are only part of the story, however. In the chapters ahead we're going to take a close look at both quantitative and qualitative data. Taken together, they provide the two sides of good (meaningful) analysis.

Quantitative data is about numbers

Quantitative data can be counted or measured. It's the kind of data we see when we look at:

- Test scores (raw numbers, pass/fail)
- Course related statistics (number of posts, learning objects completed)
- Performance measures (sales data, error rate, customer satisfaction)
- Benchmarking (gap reduction, goals met)

Numbers are useful and important, but numbers can be limiting when we seek to answer key questions around learning, such as:

- Did it work?
- What made it work?
- Who didn't it work for? Why not?

The questions that drive an effective learning design are questions that go beyond linear regression to tell the whole story. They try to step beyond correlation and into causality; they try to establish not just the "what," but the "why."

Qualitative data is descriptive

Qualitative data concerns that which cannot be measured by a meter stick, a test score, or a time on the clock. It can include:

- User feedback
- Sentiment
- Content
- demographics

Qualitative data puts metaphorical flesh on the bare bones of quantitative data. For example, if we look at text responses to a question, we can measure the word count but that won't tell us all we need to know about the quality of the responses. Analyzing the content of the responses to that same question will give us qualitative data: a sense of keywords, the degree of understanding, or the application of a concept. Or, in another scenario, we may receive a lot of positive user feedback after a course (qualitative data), but that data doesn't tell us the whole story. Users may say they liked the course, but we will need some quantitative (and possibly qualitative) performance data to determine if it was an effective course.

In later chapters we'll explore how to work with both quantitative and qualitative data and look at some basic examples of using them together in analysis. Before we think about using data, however, we need to be sure our data is capable of doing what we need it to do. We need to talk about data quality.

Data Quality

In an ideal world, all our data would be complete, consistent, readily available, and accurate. When using two (or more!) data sets together, those data sets would have perfectly matched "keys," that is, a common set of values, such as user identification, that allow us to connect data across different data sets. And of course we'd love for our data to have consistent formatting, with no duplicate or incomplete records. In reality, this isn't the case, and so when we start to do analysis, we first have to spend time finding what's inconsistent and what's missing. There's always some "data cleaning" to be done. Data quality refers to how fit a data set is for its intended purpose, according to characteristics of "completeness, validity, accuracy, consistency, availability and timeliness" (ISO 9001). In practical terms, this means we need to look at the data and see if it represents the real world accurately. We need to make sure that different data sets are aligned. In other words, do the data sets represent the same elements consistently?

For example, we may want to know how much time users spend during each visit to our eLearning portal. When we examine our data, we might note that the majority of visits last between 15 and 30 minutes, but one or two visits clock in at, say, 15 hours. Since it's unlikely that anyone has spent 15 hours continuously doing training, this alerts us that there's likely a problem in the data somewhere. Whether the problem lies in how we are set up to log user time on the portal, or something else, it's worth checking into.

When we're working with multiple data sets, data consistency is especially necessary. The data might be from different systems, or it might be data in the same system over time, and it's not uncommon to find different date or other numeric formats, different user IDs for the same person, or even different criteria for a field (for example, how we define "active user" or "time spent on portal" or even "pass").

There's no getting around the fact that we need to take a hard look at our data before analysis. We can do this through basic data exploration, like reading the raw data, counting types, and matching key-value pairs. We also need to understand thoroughly where the numbers are coming from in terms of actions, criteria, and which interactions in an application interface create which pieces of data. When we do this, the resulting analysis is likely to be more valid, more useful, and less frustrating. We will also gain knowledge about ways to improve future data collection efforts so that we will generate data that will most effectively meet our needs.

What is the minimum I need to know about data?

Once we collect (or make plans to collect) the data, we must consider how to use it well. There is a saying that goes, "Torture the data long enough and it will confess to anything." To gain meaningful insights from our data, we need to understand it well enough to use it effectively.

First questions

When we're working with quantitative data, we have to ask, what makes those numbers come into being? What are the activities or transactions behind the numbers?

We ask these questions if we want to use our data well. Knowing how data was created helps us understand what it means. For example, if we have data on "active users," how is "active" defined? Is it:

- One login a week?
- A certain amount of time spent on the course?
- A percentage of completion?

If we know the criteria, we can meaningfully interpret results. When we have specific questions, we may find that one definition gives us more useful data than another, and we'll want this to guide how we filter our data.

For example, if we discover time-based patterns for activities within a data set, we might ask, is that time normalized by location, or are all timestamps set to a single time zone regardless of the user's location? If we want to find out whether learners are more likely to access course content at certain times of day, but the timestamps in the data are all set to UTC (Coordinated Universal Time) while the learners are globally distributed, we will need to have data about learner location in order to translate time zones. Without such information the data might indicate that a lot of people access the course in the early evening, when in fact a large cohort in California is working on the course right after lunch.

Was data automatically generated or entered manually? When we account for such conditions, our analysis is more likely to yield valid results. For example, nothing propagates errors faster than a spreadsheet. And when it comes to collecting qualitative data, manual entry of data gives us flexibility. Knowing how a set of data is generated helps us know what types of issues to look for, which in turn helps us reduce frustration and wasted time.

How hard is it to get the data we want?

We might know what data we want, but this doesn't mean we can lay our hands on it. Some aspects of data are within our control and some are definitely not. This is true of data collection and also of the actions we take with our data.

There may be data that we want or need, but it's challenging or impossible to access it – for reasons of technology limitations, organizational constraints, cost, or other factors. When you work with data, you know that things will go wrong, and that things will surprise you. The more you can anticipate the issues, the more able you will be make the best use of the data you have.

In addition to issues about access to data, we need to be aware of factors that can make data easy or difficult to analyze. The first question to consider is the data format. Flat files, such as comma separated value (.csv) files are easily imported into spreadsheets, databases and other data analytics tools. If your data is in a SQL or noSQL database, you'll need to know how to query for the data you need, or you'll need access to support who can do it for you.

Whether analysis is easy will also depend on how many data sources you are working with and whether the data is formatted in ways that are compatible. You'll find that when working with multiple data sources it's common to deal with differences in the formatting of names, user identifiers, and dates. It's not a difficult problem to manage, but it takes time and attention to bring the data to a common format, while making sure that records aren't altered (or lost, or duplicated) along the way. We find it helpful to keep running notes of data sources and issues, so that we have a record of problems and the relevant processes to manage them successfully.

Of course, data collection is not necessarily or entirely in your hands. Whether you are working within or outside the learning ecosystem, you'll need to think not just about how the data is created, but about which data you'll be able to access and when and how. This means it's time to think about the supply chain.

Data Supply Chain

If we're using data to evaluate the effectiveness of learning, we need to look at people's actions and experiences outside the learning ecosystem. It's more than just a good idea – it provides a more realistic, more complete vision of what's going on. At the same time, it can be rough terrain to navigate because when we look at data outside the learning ecosystem, we are looking at data outside our control. And, realistically, even within the learning ecosystem we may have access to all or most of the data, but we may or may not have had control over how the data was collected, what definitions and criteria were set, or what format it is in. There's a lot we need to consider before we can distill the information we need from the data we can access.

Let's say we've been asked to evaluate the effectiveness of our new sales training course. In the course, the objective was to increase capability for sales of (A) through clearer articulation of the benefits of (A) for the user, with the success metric being a sales increase of N%.

How are we going to do this? We start by asking some questions:

1. What information do we need, and where will we find it?"
   o Ideal dataset to answer the question
   o Some quantitative, some qualitative
2. What is the data's availability and accessibility?
   o Look at what you don't have,
      can't collect, can't access
3. We have choices: what is or is not worth pursuing?

o   Find alternate data and/or manage gaps
4.   What are the potential Data Integration concerns?
   o   Check for validity, accuracy
   o   Check data alignment (do the data sets match up)
5.   What's our comfort zone? What's "good enough"?

Applying these questions to our sales example, we begin by considering what data is necessary and what is available:

First we have the data within our Learning Ecosystem. Probably this consists of the usual test scores and completions, but ideally we'll have more. Maybe we look at which resources were accessed the most. Maybe there were extra discussion sections or breakout groups – it might be interesting to look at the participation in those. At the end of the day we want to know if the course helped lead to the desired outcome, but we can learn a lot, too, if we can start building a picture of what aspects of the course, or what paths through the course, correlate with the greatest effect.

If our metric of success is based on sales increase for a specific product, we'll need data from outside the Learning Ecosystem.

Specifically, we will want sales data. In this case we might look at 2-4 years of sales history and going forward. And we need to decide how we're going to measure sales increases (units, revenue, margin, by salesperson). Or perhaps the performance metric has been pre-determined. Either way, we need to know what we're measuring against. We need to know what data we have access to. We need to look at how it's formatted, where it comes from, and how the various data fields are defined.

We might also decide that it would be useful to evaluate how effectively the salespeople who participated in the course describe the value proposition of (A). Is there a way to do this without affecting their behavior or performance? If a supervisor is doing the assessment, will there be bias or personality conflicts that skew the data? What about a survey of customers and prospective customers, to gain insight into salespeople's communication before and after the course? Such a survey would give useful information, but what would the trade-offs be? If we conducted a third-party blind survey so that the information we received was anonymized it might offer insights for the overall cohort of course participants, but not for individual performance.

Do we have alternate sources of data that might give us similar information? Can we look at our customer support data and see if there's a trend that would indicate improved communication of the product's value proposition? Did a greater percentage of people end up being sold the right thing?

General performance across a cohort might be all we need or want to know, but if our analysis goals call for learner-specific performance data, things can become more complicated. For example, we might need to examine the HR implications. At a minimum, HR would need to be involved the process. And do we have the time and resources for that?

After weighing data analysis goals against available data, data limitations and the resource costs of different approaches against the value of the information generated, it's a matter of making decisions. What information is critical, what can you live without, and what can you compensate for with other approaches? It's always a balancing act, but one way to manage it is to do some of the simplest analyses first; these results will often give a better sense of what (if any) more complex efforts should follow.

In this sales training case, it's pretty likely that quantitative learning data and sales data will be accessible and usable. And that data may well be sufficient for establishing the behavioral impact of a course. Yet in this case we're looking at sales performance in a bit of a vacuum; our closed system contains only the course results and sales performance. It basically assumes no other significant contributing factors. That may or may not be a safe assumption to make. Is our analysis too simple? We'll dig more deeply into how to approach real-world analysis in Chapters 10 and 11.

There may be other variables that need testing. It is important to know what level of precision is called for; it is also important to know when something seemingly trivial is a critical data point.

The need for both quantitative and qualitative

In the next couple of chapters we'll be taking an in-depth look at qualitative and quantitative data. Even in the simple example described above, regression analysis would probably not provide the whole story. If we want to look more deeply into correlation and begin to explore causality, using both types of data is a powerful tool – pointing to both the what and the why.

In a scenario where we measured the value of objects in a MOOC, we explored a number of quantitative observations: counts of object views, time spent on objects, comments, replies to comments. If the course had included formal assessments we could have looked for correlation between object completion and assessment results. All of this would have given some insight as to which objects were used and created some sort of reaction. And this would have been a decent first pass, but where it actually got interesting was when we started digging into the comments and saw some very strong reactions to certain objects – some positive, some definitely not. This prompted us to look for trends in terms of which users did, or did not, like specific objects. As a result, we discovered a strong division of preferences for object types with respect to formats, media type and length – with preferences clearly aligned to functional roles. From a designer's standpoint, this was a useful insight drawn from a fairly simple combination of data types.

In the next couple of chapters, we'll explore quantitative and qualitative data in more depth, before moving on to analysis.

References

Ambler, Scott. "Data Modeling 101." Agile Data. Accessed January 26, 2017. www.agiledata.org/essays/dataModeling101.html.

DuMoulin, Rob. "Where Data Governance Stops and Master Data Management Starts | Hub Designs Magazine." Hub Designs Magazine. Accessed January 26, 2017. https://hubdesignsmagazine.com/2011/10/13/where-data-governance-stops-and-master-data-management-starts/.

Duvall, Erik. "Attention Please! Learning Analytics for Visualization and Recommendation." Proceedings of the 1st International Conference on Learning Analytics and Knowledge, LAK '11. Last modified 2011. https://lirias.kuleuven.be/bitstream/123456789/315113/1/.

Duvall, Laura. "Jump Starting Data Governance: a Program Manager's Story." MIT Information Quality. Last modified July 2011. http://mitiq.mit.edu/IQIS/Documents/CDOIQS_201177/Papers/02_04_1C-1_Duvall.pdf.

Dylan, William. *Embedded Formative Assessment.* Bloomington, IN: Solution Tree Press, 2011.

Elias, Tanya. "Learning Analytics - Definitions, Processes, Potential." Learning Analytics. Last modified 2011. http://learninganalytics.net/LearningAnalyticsDefinitionsProcessesPotential.pdf.

Macfadyen, Leah P., and Shane Dawson. "Numbers Are Not Enough. Why e-Learning Analytics Failed to Inform an Institutional Strategic Plan." Journal of Educational Technology & Society. Last modified 2012. http://ifets.info/journals/15_3/11.pdf.

Siemens, George, and Ryan S. Baker. "Learning Analytics and Educational Data Mining: Towards Communication and Collaboration." Worcester Polytechnic Institute. Accessed January 26, 2017. http://users.wpi.edu/~rsbaker/LAKs%20reformatting%20v2.pdf.

University of California, Berkely. "Data Analysis Toolkits." UC Berkeley Seismology Lab. Accessed January 29, 2017. http://seismo.berkeley.edu/~kirchner/eps_120/EPSToolkits.htm.

West Virginia University. "WVU Study Found Elevated Levels of Emissions from Volkswagen Vehicles." WVUToday. Last modified September 24, 2015. http://wvutoday.wvu.edu:8002/n/2015/09/24/wvu-study-found-elevated-levels-of-emissions-from-volkswagen-vehicles.

Chapter 4

Qualitative Data

In this chapter we take a closer look at what qualitative data is and how it is collected. A typical scenario will help us define qualitative data: A set of eLearning modules is developed and deployed to the target audience. Basic statistics (data) from the modules have been reviewed. Learners are accessing the modules, but not the way you thought they would. Why? This is extremely hard to determine from raw numbers. Looking at the number of learners accessing the modules does not explain why they are using them in a certain way. To get to the "why," we need qualitative data. This chapter describes tactics for gathering more information on why they are doing what they are doing. We will also look at where qualitative data can be collected earlier in the design process.

What Is Qualitative Data?

What is qualitative data and where does it comes from? In simplest terms, qualitative data is data that cannot be quantified. It is something that does not have a number associated to it. It is not the number of learners, for example, that visited a web page. Qualitative data is the demographics of the learners that visited the page, or how the learners feel about the page. For example, let's consider a survey that asks learners to rate the page on a scale of 1 to 5 for usability or design. While the 1 to 5 scale produces numbers that can be associated to the qualitative data, those numbers mean something different to every person. So we cannot simply describe the results using the numbers.

Why Collect Qualitative Data?

While quantitative data – which we will attend to in more detail later – shows us counts and can help us construct a timeline, qualitative data helps show why learners took a certain path or what they found useful in a piece of content. Qualitative data is subjective by nature. It will vary depending on the background and experiences of the participants. We don't often talk about demographics when we talk about data, but demographics play a large role in how learners approach problems. Too often, demographics are not considered when we think about why learners behave a certain way. Demographics, such as education level, work background, and previous experiences, play a significant role in how learners interact with content. Guidelines might attempt to tell learners how to go about answering a series of questions, but ultimately their perceptions and experiences will come into play. These perceptions and experiences help explain their behavior.

It is important to understand the role that qualitative data plays in the analysis of quantitative data. Qualitative data plays a crucial role when we analyze deployed content – when we are looking at why and how a course performs for the learner taking it. We want to understand why the learners are performing the way they are and how that affects course outcomes. We don't simply want to know the outcomes of the assessment, but what led to those outcomes. In test scores, we can see patterns, but more analysis is needed to see exactly what happened to generate those scores. Qualitative data is an effective tool to help complete the picture. In later chapters we will discuss using data to close the feedback loop and make intelligent design decisions based on the data.

A case study on the importance of qualitative data

Let's look at a case study that can be found in David and Tom Kelley's book *Creative Confidence*. The case study involves two Stanford graduate students, Akshay Kothari and Ankit Gupta, who enrolled in the d.school. The d.school's culminating course is called LaunchPad. The course asks students to start a company from scratch and incorporate by the end of the quarter. Kothari and Gupta decided to create an app for the iPad that would help learners read the daily news. They needed to have a functioning app in a very short timeframe (10 weeks). The first assignment gave them four days to build a prototype. They needed quick feedback on the design and functions of the app. In that short time frame the two students spent up to 10 hours per day at a local coffee shop collecting qualitative data. The coffee shop setting allowed them to perform research with a lot of participants drawn from the target audience. They started with rough prototypes that could be updated very quickly. They spent time with patrons of the coffee shop, showing them the prototype and collecting their feedback. The initial prototype started as Post-it notes that simulated the user interface. The feedback from this provided the initial research into the design of the interface. They were able to use these quick prototypes to build a functional software prototype. The prototype was loaded onto an iPad and was then tested further among the patrons of the coffee shop. The pair observed (a qualitative data collection method) how learners interacted with the app. They took the data they collected and made as many as a hundred changes to the app design and functions within a given day. Everything in the application was open to change, depending on the data collected. In two weeks they went from something that learners didn't want to use to something that learners wanted to know, did it come pre-loaded on the iPad? The end result was Pulse News, which was shown by Steve Jobs at an Apple developer conference while Kothari and Gupta were still students and later purchased by LinkedIn. The application was built and tested by collecting qualitative data from the patrons of the coffee shop and using that data to drive the design and functions of the app. Even when it was rough, the data collected proved to be invaluable to the creation and ultimately the success of the app. Using the data to iterate quickly allowed them to create the final design in a short period of time. This case study is an example of how getting in front of learners and collecting qualitative data can lead to great, data-driven design. We see the value of qualitative data, and in a later chapter we will talk more about the feedback loop for making design changes based on data.

Methods for Collecting Qualitative Data

There are many ways to collect qualitative data. The method of choice is going to be dictated by the situation. It may even be a combination of different collection methods. Each method can be used at any time during the design process, from early in the prototyping phase to measuring the outcomes of a deployed intervention.

Participant Observation

Participant observation as a method of collecting qualitative data presents certain challenges. It means that the data collector embeds him or herself into the role or culture of the learners being researched. Depending on what is being researched, this can take months or years to complete. The data is collected among participants in their "natural" state. The researcher is not seen as an outsider, but as someone who is part of normal day-to-day operations. Because the researcher is part of the collection process, this method takes far too long for most projects. For this reason we will move on to other methods.

Direct Observation

The direct observation method is similar to participant observation with one huge difference: the data collector does not try to embed him or herself in the process or culture of the group being studied. The collector tries to be as unobtrusive as possible but is not a piece of the process. The observer watches and takes notes on what is taking place. We will talk in a later chapter about ways to use technology for this type of observation.

A second big distinction with direct observation is the focus of what is being studied. In direct observation, the data collector typically applies a narrow focus to a certain piece of a process. In the context of what we're discussing, it might be the interface of a module, a piece of content, or a set of screens that will be in a module. The narrow focus allows for situations to be set up and observed without having to worry about the entire process or all situations. Another important distinction is the length of time needed for direct observation. It is far less than the time needed for participant observation.

Observing Learners

Observing learners can be a critical part of qualitative data collection when we're talking about designing interfaces or content. Observing user's interactions can start very early in the design process. When doing physical prototyping of any kind it's great to get end learners' feedback early in the process. Useful early feedback on the design comes from watching how they work the interface and the elements within. For example, we might watch their facial expressions and how their hands move across the interface. First, though, we need a consistent method to explain the interface to the learners and convey what it is supposed to accomplish. Using a consistent method will ensure that each learner is starting from the same point. If different learners receive different explanations, they could take different things from the testing which could skew the feedback. One idea is to write scenarios for the learners that assign them to certain roles. The scenario provides a common theme that can be used with multiple learners and ensures that everyone is starting at the same point. These scenarios may differ between groups that are being tested. We could write a scenario that focuses on the overall module design. Meanwhile, for target learners we could write scenarios that focus on key roles that might come into play. The scenario will reflect the group we are working with. The scenario might look at items such as long travel times, how far the hand or "mouse" moves between elements, and how confusion or frustration come into play. In this phase of testing it is probably a good idea to have two people monitor sessions – one takes notes on how the test subjects react to the interface while the other watches for travel distances and takes notes on that. A video camera can record learners using the physical prototype, which generates a record of what happened during the session. (A camera also helps if a second person is not available to help run the test session.) At minimum, observers should take detailed notes about where the test subjects run into issues as they work through the interface. Observing learners is a great method for editing deployed content, especially when paired with quantitative data collected from the intervention. After we analyze data and spot an issue, observing learners is an effective way to collect some qualitative data to confirm or deny the hypothesis as to why an intervention is or is not working.

In all of the examples we've just mentioned, we will need to generate a representative cross section of the group for which the intervention is built. Using a representative group ensures that we get a representative data sample. If we focus too much on a single group, we might end up building something that is not usable by other groups. Stakeholders can help define the groups that need to be represented. We can also get information to help define representative samples from a case study or needs analysis if available.. During the documentation of a process, the groups, and their roles in the process, should become clear.

Interviews

When collecting qualitative data, two types of interview methods are available: unstructured and structured Each type has characteristics that make it valuable.

Unstructured interviews are typically free-flowing interviews with some initial questions or guiding principles. The interview can proceed from there based on the intuition of the interviewer and how the interviewee answers questions. The fact that there is no rigid setup allows the topic to end up being broader than anticipated. It can help uncover information that the interviewer was not looking for – which can be good and bad, depending on the situation.

An unstructured interview requires the interviewer to have a deep knowledge of the subject and often requires a good rapport with the interviewee. A strong knowledge of the subject matter will help the interviewer ask the right questions to dig into the subject. A good rapport will, hopefully, open up the interviewee to delve deeper into the subject matter. If we're using this method we need to be cautious, because with little structure the interview can stray into areas that are not relevant to the topic. We might also find that it becomes difficult to group information collected from unstructured interviews. Since the interviewer has no set list of questions, each interview will be a little bit different. Without a defined list of questions, the grouping becomes more difficult as the answers won't follow a set pattern of questions. If conducting unstructured interviews, it is good to note patterns that happen within the interview – this might help guide subsequent interviews in a way that will make it easier to apply more logical groupings in the data collected.

Structured interviews use a strict set of questions asked of all participants. Using the same questions for each person provides a logical grouping of the data that is being collected. Since the questions are the same, patterns can emerge from the data allowing the results to be more easily categorized. Structured interviews can be led by anyone who can be trained to give the interview. The interviews are easy to duplicate because the questions are asked in the same sequence to all participants. Their advantage is that they tend to be quick, but they are also very rigid. Since the questions are asked the same way every time, there is no room for additional questions.

Interviews of any kind can be a difficult method of collecting data. Learners are not always forthright in interviews. You are asking learners to remember what took place when they were trying out an interface. It is possible that they will not remember everything that happened as it happened. It is not that the learner is being dishonest; it is simply the way the brain works. Their biases come into play, and they focus on different things when working through the content. Another phenomenon that can skew interview results is learners giving answers that they think the interviewer wants to hear. Perhaps the learner doesn't want to hurt feelings by saying something was bad, so they say it was OK. Later in this chapter we will talk about how direct observation can help alleviate such situations. Not all biases belong to the interviewee; the interviewer, too, can introduce biases. This might be something as simple as the interviewer's body language while asking the questions, but it can affect the answers that are given. Interviewers need to avoid conveying an opinion while asking questions and need to be aware of their own body language and tone when asking questions.

Case Studies

Case studies are typically a combination of the above methods. You combine research methods to come up with answers to the questions you want answered. With a case study, you can go very deep and study specific things at a detailed level. Case studies tend to take a long time, but they provide thorough output of the group being studied. In learning intervention design, you might perform a case study prior to building content. From a case study you would obtain in-depth knowledge of a group's process and needs. A case study can also be thought of as a needs analysis. Interviewing learners can help you document the processes and map them to the behaviors that you are trying to change. The case study could then be combined with surveys to determine how current processes are working. Once you understand what the learners are trying to do and how it is working, you can develop a picture of what needs to change and how to begin building the intervention to change it.

Surveys

Surveys can be used to collect data from a set of subjects. Surveys will normally take written form. They can ask learners for short answers or use a rating scale to gain feedback. A rating scale allows learners to relate how they feel about something in numerical form. The main issue with this type of rating system is that it is very subjective. A 3 out of 5 will mean something completely different to each learner taking the survey. So in many cases short-answer questions can be used to gain some context. If there are no short answers, we can gain context by interviewing the subject. Context is key when using a survey. A number on a rating scale means nothing if we have no details about what is behind it. It is also the case that learners tend to rate things higher when taking a survey. They don't want to be too critical of the item that is being reviewed.

What To Measure

There are many types of tests we can run if we want to collect qualitative data. They can be as simple as a survey and can go as far as observing users in action. When we collect qualitative data, we are collecting subjective, opinion-based data. Smile sheets are a common example. Did you enjoy the course? How do you rate it on a scale of 1 to 5? Did the instructor keep your attention? How many times did you fall asleep? (Yes, that last question is quantitative, but you get the idea.) Qualitative data can't be quantified in numbers. It consists of feelings and opinions based on content and background.

The collection methods we've described are available for use at any time during the design and deployment process. A combination of methods can be used to produce the data needed. After collecting the data, it is important to organize and code the data. We need to form the data into logical groups. Examples are: education, job role, reasons for needing a course (required, voluntary, combination of both), and there are many other potential organization factors depending on the situation. Once we have some logical organization, we need to read and code the collected data carefully. Coding data means categorizing the data logically and systematically. All data in a category must have something that ties it all together, and the created categories should be clearly differentiated from one another. Furthermore, no data should be left outside of the categories. Every project is unique when it comes to organizing and coding data, and it takes some practice to become adept at working with qualitative data.

Collect Qualitative Data Earlier

Qualitative data is great for prototyping and user testing. These are things we can't quantify with a number because no consistent numerical scale exists that will give results. If you ask someone how he or she feels, even on a scale that is the same from person to person, each person is going to have a different idea of what the scale means. The scale is open for interpretation by the test subjects. If we ask them to rate a design on a scale of 1 to 5 and tell them that 1 means "outstanding" and 5 means "awful," those levels are open to interpretation. They are going to mean different things to everyone that takes the survey. There is no right answer, no right way to interpret the scale. Interpreting the type of data collected can then be difficult for the researcher. Therefore, as we will discuss later, it is a good idea to include a second collection method: to talk with the learners who took the survey. Using a combination of collection methods allows us to gather information on the way the survey was interpreted. When we add this information to the survey, it makes the data usable and puts it in context. Without context, we will have a hard time finding usable results in the data collected.

Unfortunately, too often we either don't collect any qualitative data or we collect it too late. We should be looking to collect and use qualitative data earlier in the design process. In fact, many industries are already doing this. If we look at the app design process, for example, we see a lot of user testing being done in the early stages to design the interface. During prototyping the design team can get feedback from learners on how the interface looks and feels, and this feedback is invaluable to getting the design "right." Web design also uses qualitative data when designing web pages. Getting feedback on placement of items, colors, and element size defines the page design. By working with the potential end-user, the designers get great feedback about how potential end-learners will perceive their design.

References

Aycan, David and Paolo Lorenzoni. 2014. "The Human Element In Digital Prototyping". Harvard Business Review. http://blogs. hbr.org/2014/05/good-digital-prototyping-takes-empathy-2/?utm_source=Socialflow&utm_medium=Tweet&utm_campaign=Socialflow.

Cao, Jerry. 2016. "The Practical Beginner'S Guide To User Research". Studio By Uxpin. https://studio.uxpin.com/blog/the-practical-beginners-guide-to-user-research/?utm_source=twitter&utm_medium=uxlink&utm_campaign=&utm_content=blog.

Kelley, David and Tom Kelley. Creative Confidence.

Mayring, Philipp. 2000. "Qualitative Content Analysis". Forum Qualitative Sozialforschung / Forum: Qualitative Social Research 1 (2). http://www.qualitative-research. net/index.php/fqs/article/viewArticle/1089/2385.

Rohrer, Christian. 2014. "When To Use Which User-Experience Research Methods". Nngroup.Com. http://www. nngroup.com/articles/which-ux-research-methods/.

Wondrack, James. 2015. "A Common Design Taxonomy | UX Magazine". Uxmag.Com. http://uxmag.com/articles/a-common-design-taxonomy?utm_source=feedblitz&utm_medium=FeedBlitzRss&utm_campaign=uxm.

O'Sullivan-Munck, Jessica. 2013. "Gathering Website Data For Successful Analysis". Siteimprove. http://siteimprove.com/blog/gathering-website-data/.

Chapter 5

Quantitative Data

In the previous chapter we looked at qualitative data as the tool to answer the "why" questions. In this chapter we will explore using quantitative data is to answer "what" or "how many" questions. Quantitative data is numeric; it is measures and counts, and we can apply mathematical operations to the numbers to get meaningful answers.

What Is Quantitative Data?

Quantitative data is often our brains' default assumption when we hear the word "data." It's counting clicks, it's adding up time, it's scores, as examples. It is more familiar turf than qualitative data, if only because, historically, it has been the type of data that's readily available without extra effort. We can get our hands on it and display it in a graph or spreadsheet.

Unfortunately, this ease of access can turn out to be a double-edged sword. When we access and use the data in ways that are so familiar, there is the potential to use it thoughtlessly, to easily and unconsciously default to the kinds of answers and analysis we've always done. This include test scores, completions, time spent on site, etc

Why Collect Quantitative Data?

A lifetime of schooling and the historically limited availability of data have trained us to treat numbers as scorecards. We apply basic calculations and get basic answers about completions or average time spent, or whatever it is we've been asked to measure. It's a good place to start, but generally it's not the best place to stop. Taking a pure accounting approach to quantitative data can be useful and important, but it's not sufficient if we want to realize the full information potential of our data. We want to collect and analyze learning data to obtain insights more useful than just "pass" rates.

If we are investing the time and effort to work with learning data, we are most likely looking to use that data strategically: to inform decisions, guide actions, and support improvements. That being the case, we need to approach the collection and analysis of quantitative data with our goals in mind, selecting data to meet our information needs, rather than selecting our analyses based on the data at hand.

In order to know where to start with the wealth of data available, we need to ask some questions:

- What are we going to measure?
- What behavior are we trying to change?
- How do we measure success?
- What are we doing anyway?

What Are We Going To Measure?

The simplest starting point to determine our goals is to ask who needs this data, and why?

Perhaps the HR department wants to know if the sales training worked. Or L&D wants to see if the design changes in a course have made it easier for people to find the elements they need. Perhaps the organization's leaders are wondering what the participation and completion rates are, and if those rates correlate to meeting performance goals.

When we think about goals, we can consider what information the stakeholders (or data customers) need to help them make decisions or evaluations around their goals. The more specifically we can identify the information goals, the more likely we are to collect the data needed to meet those goals.

In the real world this often boils down to a stakeholder simply wanting to know, "Did this work?," or "What is our return on investment for this course?"

If the goal is to determine whether a course is "effective," we might look more closely at whether specific parts of the course are more effective than others. We would also want to consider the actions or decisions that may result from this information and consider what stakeholders need to know to make the best decisions. If we consider not just the stated information request but the goals or intentions behind that request, we are much more likely to collect a useful data set on the first pass.

When we are asked to demonstrate ROI the question can feel like a loaded one, but it can be a useful one if we get to the root of the question and put our data to work for us. As much as it seems as though this question is asking us to think like accountants, it's actually giving us an opportunity to think like analysts.

This is a golden opportunity for demonstrating the value of L&D, and if we can design our data collection and deliver our message within the relevant business context we can take the ROI discussion beyond a tally sheet and into some meaningful exploration of learning and development. It would be ideal, of course, if we could just get people to see the world through our lens and grasp the value that learning can offer, but in reality we have customers for our L&D and customers for our L&D data, who may or may not be the same people, with their own pressures and needs. If we ask the right questions, we can meet or exceed their expectations, and we can often address several information needs from a single data set.

The good news is that the main skill you need to plan data collection and analysis is one that learning professionals already have: being proficient at asking questions, and lots of them.

- Who needs this data? Why? Who else?

- What do they really need to know? Be specific.
- What outside factors will influence response to this data? Again, be specific.
- At what organizational level or functional role will we be making decisions or taking actions based on this data?

This last question is key: if we want to deliver something actionable, the data we need to collect and how we analyze it is highly context-dependent. The data we need for strategic or tactical level decisions (e.g. value analysis within the context of organizational goals) is going to differ from the data needed for operational level decisions (e.g. is this performance need better addressed with a job aid or a course?).

Donald Clark has broken down the typical functional levels for learning data into a 10-Level Taxonomy. For most organizational learning, our data focus is generally on one or more of the following levels:

Learners

By understanding what does and does not work for individual learners, or for populations of learners, we gain valuable insight that can allow us to examine the course with an eye toward supporting specific needs and interests. Data at the learner level can be used to examine learning paths, create individual recommendations based on similar users or based on performance (e.g. novice > expert mapping), or create more meaningful branched learning or scenario-based learning.

Course Components

Looking at course components in isolation can be a bit of an exercise in bean-counting, but looking at them in context can provide a wealth of insight about what's working and what isn't. With quantitative data we can examine a number of details that tell us a lot about how people interact with our courses and what elements provide value for them, with questions such as:

- What generates interaction, conversation, reflection?
- What did people struggle with?
- What did people ignore? Did it matter?
- How long will people pay attention to different media types?
- Do different roles/regions respond differently to different types of activities?
- Were people who completed A measurably more successful at B?

This sort of data can provide a lot of value in the context of organizational performance needs assessments and goal achievement measures. It's also a place where opportunities abound for course design improvements.

Courses

Similarly we can look at course data in context. With carefully collected data, we can look at more than just the percentage of those enrolled who completed the course or passed their assessment. We can look at how the course is performing. If everyone is struggling or there is a high proportion of non-completion, we might want to dig deeper, to find out whether there are places the course lacks clarity, is too advanced or too simple, or is not relevant or necessary. We might ask, Is there a tipping point where people either continue or quit? If so, can we determine why?

We can also start to examine whether the course is having the desired effect. Can we draw correlations between completion (or completion up to a certain point) and performance goals achieved?

Groups of Courses

When we're trying to change complex behaviors, or build capabilities that call for cumulative knowledge, or effect a change in business process, a single short-term course won't have much to say about whether an impact has occurred. If we are exploring value provided or considering big-picture questions such as trends in participation, we will need to look at groups of courses.

This might apply, too, if we're trying to understand general principles of learner interactions with our courses, or what participation factors (objects completed, levels completed, community engagement, etc.) correlate with successful completion rates.

Institutions or Organizations

At the organizational level, we may be investigating questions of where and how L&D makes a difference overall.

- Are completion rates improving for our courses?
- Is there a correlation between course completions and professional advancement or retention?
- Are we seeing the intended business process improvements (e.g. has there been a reduction in forecast errors) or behavioral changes (are we seeing an increase in quality and efficiency in responding to customer complaints)?

What Behavior Are We Trying to Change?

When we're designing learning interventions we're usually working in one of a few areas:

- **Informational** – new knowledge/understanding
  o New products, techniques, procedures
- **Behavioral (Micro)** – individual habits, actions, or skills
  o Personal professional development, management training
- **Behavioral (Macro)** – large-scale process or procedural changes across business units and/or across long time spans
  o Business process improvement

The types of questions we need to answer, and hence the types of data we will need, will vary depending on the learning goals. If we're looking at a short course that aims to develop coaching skills for new managers, we're going to have different measures of success and a different data set than we would for a year-long project to develop improved supply chain processes.

Additionally, our ability to measure effects will be dependent on the scale (personal versus organizational) and the timeframe of what is being attempted. For learning that involves more complex process changes, we will probably need to look at development across a series of courses. And we need to recognize that the effectiveness of what has been learned may not appear in performance results for several months after the course is complete. Individual efforts are part of a system, so the net effects will have a specific business life cycle before they can be observed.

Selecting relevant data sets and data time ranges will depend on what questions we need to answer. The primary question remains:

- Did it work?

But we need to break that down into some more specific questions:

- Did people take the course?
- Did they respond to it by . . .
  - scoring well
  - writing reflections
  - engaging in conversation
  - sharing links
  - uploading videos, etc.?
- Did their work in the course change their actions on the job?
- Did the course actually matter? Did the changes deliver the intended benefits?

We need to be looking for the right data sets, in the right time frames, to answer the right questions.

How Do We Measure Success?

To measure success we have to define success. A meaningful definition is one that looks beyond the boundaries of the course. If we dig into the reasons behind a course or learning intervention, we ultimately find that the defining terms can be expressed by a fundamental business measure:

How Do We Tie This to the Bottom Line?

This is not always a simple question to answer. Depending on the situation, the bottom line is likely to be something that cannot be measured solely on an accounting spreadsheet. For a medical facility, a course regardless of the topic might be tied to improving patient outcomes; individual courses might contribute to various aspects of that goal, whether the courses are designed to decrease waiting times for treatment or improve disease-prevention measures. When looking at customer-facing roles in a service organization, we might want to know how a course on effective management of complaints improves the rate of repeat customers or referrals. This means we need to be attuned to what the overall bottom line need is and how a particular course or group of courses fits into the specific learning ecosystem.

Even in the case of sales training, where the definition of the bottom line and measures of success might seem obvious, it's worth doing some deeper thinking as we consider what data to collect and analyze.

For example, a company wants to increase the sales of (Product/Service), and it knows that a key factor in sales increases is the ability to understand customer needs, and it articulates the value proposition of the appropriate offering to meet those needs. To understand if the course has helped achieve this goal, we may want a variety of data both internal and external to the course:

- **Success in course** – This is the obvious one. Did people participate in the course, complete it, perform well in it (based on how you've defined course performance)?
- **Success in elements of the course** – It's worthwhile to go to

a higher level of detail. We may find that certain elements of a course have a stronger impact on performance than others, or that some work better for different populations. This helps us to iterate and improve course design.

- **Customer feedback** – If we want to know if salespeople are better at articulating the value proposition of a product, customers are our firsthand source of information. They can also give insights about what they need, which can be integrated into future design.
- **Sales cycle** – We need to know the sales cycle of products. If something has a typical six-month time frame from customer meeting to final sale, then measuring sales impacts one or three months after course completion won't tell us anything.
- **Seasonality** – Is the offering a seasonal one? If so, it will affect how you measure performance impact.
- **Environment (economic, competitive)** – A new competing product or service in the market may affect sales overall. Knowing this allows you to measure more accurately whether the course changed sales.

This is just one example, but the takeaway is that we need more than test scores and sales figures if we want to answer critical questions about a learning activity or course:

- Did it work?
- What parts of it worked?
- How much of a difference did it make?
- How can we make it better?

How Do We Know What We Need?

Our first step toward answering our stakeholders' questions – and our own questions, for that matter – is to determine the data we need. One way we can begin to do this is by taking a page from the playbook of business strategists and riffing off the Balanced Scorecard.

The Balanced Scorecard helps keep track of the activities and outcomes within a business by examining both financial and non-financial elements and then evaluating them within the context of the strategic goals of the organization, its stakeholders, and customers. Similarly with learning we can use balanced measures. Potentially, this can involve course data and other performance data, viewed in the context of specific strategic goals of the stakeholders, the learners, and/or the instructional design team.

When we're evaluating the effectiveness of a course, it's useful to look at both leading and trailing measures of effectiveness and success. Leading measures are those which predict performance, whereas trailing measures document what has happened. As an example, if I'm trying to lose weight, stepping on the scale at the end of the week is a trailing measure – it tells me something about what I did already. A food diary and data from my fitness tracker are leading measures – predictors of what I'm likely to see at the weekly weigh-in.

As we improve our data collection practices, we'll be able to start looking at the leading measures (formative) rather than just the trailing (summative). In a course or series of courses, leading measures might include: time spent, number of sessions, conversations, uploads, contributions, and progress through the course. Trailing measures would include: scores, follow-up, and performance data. Over time we can learn what leading activities lead to successful performance and which parts of the course or other activities make a difference.

This is very powerful; it can allow us to be aware of when learners are struggling and need some support. It's also an opportunity to measure the course, not just the learners.

So What Does This Look Like in Real Life?

Honestly, it looks like a lot of trial and error, and sometimes it involves good luck, when we happen to add one more piece of data or ask one more question from a new angle.

Fortunately for data collection purposes, the business

questions we are trying to answer – regardless of how complex they are – generally fall into two main categories: questions of participation and of performance.

Typical Questions	Relevant Data
Participation Related	
What are course results?	results: completions; scores; participation (drill down to region/business unit/functional level)
Are people using the courses/tools? (e.g. What are rates of participation? Level of engagement?)	participation;* comments; replies/upvotes; shared resources/UGC; popular content; time spent;* vid views/pauses; % active
Does specific content affect course results?	resources used; results
What content affects course participation/completion?	results; participation e.g. looking for trends and/or correlations

Performance Related	
Are we teaching the right things?	user-created content and responses; novice expert actions; completions; pre-post test
How does course performance correspond to job performance?	results; participation; external data
Did X have the desired effect on Y? (e.g. did Sales Course N correspond with increase in rate of upselling as determined by Z)	content completed; results; external data

How Do We Collect Qualitative Data?

When we're collecting learning data, the first issue is one of accessibility. What data can we actually get from the LMS, LRS, as well as actual performance data?

Additionally we need to be looking at what activities or performance elements (inside and outside of courses) are actually measurable. Availability and measurability (observability) can quickly constrain what data we will be collecting and analyzing.

It shouldn't take long to identify your desired data set relative to what data is available to you and home in on what you'll actually be able to work with.

It's helpful to map out the data availability and the formats in which you'll be receiving it. This lets you anticipate how you'll need to work to get it ready for analysis. It's also good to anticipate any potential bottlenecks in your data supply chain and to consider how you'll mitigate concerns presented by other data owners (HR, managers). Your data is going to come in a lot of formats, and with differing levels of detail. In the later chapters on analysis, we'll delve more deeply into how to manage that. For now it's enough to consider what data you'll get and what it's likely to look like from a content perspective.

For example, from xAPI the types of data you might get include:

Actor	Verb	Object	Context	Result
Identifier	Attempted	Quiz	Time	Score
Role	Completed	Module	Duration	Success
Cohort	Viewed	Video	Group	Passed
	Initialized	Course	Course	Completed
	Opened	Resource		
	Contributed	Link		
	Commented			

And if you remember only one thing from this chapter, remember this:

The real value of learning data is that it allows us to assess the course as much or more than it allows us to assess the learners. It's that simple. And it's that complicated.

In the chapters on analysis we'll explore not just some basic processes, but also the questions that let us learn from our data instead of imposing our expectations on it:

- What does the data really mean?
- When ought it apply (or not) to individuals?
- When is it more appropriately applied to populations or courses?
- What are we really trying to prove or understand with a particular data set?

References

Ambler, Scott. "Data Modeling 101." Agile Data. Accessed January 26, 2017. www.agiledata.org/essays/dataModeling101.html.

Angrist, Joshua David, and Jörn-Steffen Pischke. *Mostly Harmless Econometrics: An Empiricist's Companion.* Princeton: Princeton University Press, 2009.

Barista, David. "The Big Data Revolution: How Data-driven Design is Transforming Project Planning." Building Design + Construction. Last modified February 12, 2014. https://www.bdcnetwork.com/big-data-revolution-how-data-driven-design-transforming-project-planning.

Clark, Donald. "Big Data: Ten Level Taxonomy in Learning." Donald Clark Plan B. Accessed January 26, 2017. http://donaldclarkplanb.blogspot.co.uk/2013/11/big-data-ten-level-taxonomy-in-learning.html.

Few, Stephen. *Information Dashboard Design Displaying Data for at-a-Glance Monitoring.* Burlingame, California: Analytics press, 2013.

Fleisher, Craig S., and Babette E. Bensoussan. *Business and Competitive Analysis: Effective Application of New and Classic Methods.* Upper Saddle River, NJ: Financial Times Press, 2007.

Fleisher, Craig S., and Sheila Wright. "Causes of Competitive Analysis Failure: Understanding and Responding to Problems at the Individual Level." DORA Home. Last modified 2009. https://www.dora.dmu.ac.uk/bitstream/handle/2086/4518/2009%20-%20ECIS%20Conference%20Paper%20-%20Analyst%20Failure%20FINAL.pdf?sequence=1.

Foreman, John W. *Data Smart: Using Data Science to Transform Information into Insight.* Indianapolis: John Wiley & Sons, 2014.

Fournier, Helene, Rita Kop, and Hanan Sitlia. "The Value of Learning Analytics to Networked Learning on a Personal Learning Environment." NRC Publications Archive - National

Research Council Canada / Archives Des Publications Du CNRC - Conseil National De Recherches Canada. Last modified 2011. http://nparc.cisti-icist.nrc-cnrc.gc.ca/eng/view/accepted/?id=7eb5062a-701b-480f-9b10-ec96d72c04b3.

Harnett, Donald L., and Ashok Soni. *Statistical methods for business and economics*. Reading, Mass. [etc.]: Addison-Wesley, 1991.

Laane Effron, Janet. "The Right Questions to Ask When Getting Started with Learning Data." HT2 Labs. Last modified February 9, 2016. https://www.ht2labs.com/blog/asking-why-questions-of-learning-data/.

Laane Effron, Janet. "Why Are We Doing This? Asking the Right Questions of Your Learning Data." HT2 Labs. Last modified May 18, 2016. https://www.ht2labs.com/blog/asking-right-questions-learning-data/.

Liebowitz, Jay. *Strategic Intelligence: Business Intelligence, Competitive Intelligence, and Knowledge Management*. Boca Raton: Auerbach Publications, 2006.

Loshin, David. "Data Governance for Master Data Management and Beyond." Analytics, Business Intelligence and Data Management | SAS. Accessed January 26, 2017. http://www.sas.com/content/dam/SAS/en_us/doc/whitepaper1/data-governance-for-MDM-and-beyond-105979.pdf.

Macfadyen, Leah P., and Shane Dawson. "Numbers Are Not Enough. Why e-Learning Analytics Failed to Inform an Institutional Strategic Plan." Journal of Educational Technology & Society. Last modified 2012. http://ifets.info/journals/15_3/11.pdf.

Provost, Foster, and Tom Fawcett. *Data Science for Business What You Need to Know About Data Mining and Data-Analytic Thinking*. Sebastopol: O'Reilly Media, 2013.

Riddle, Ryan. "Unlocking the Power of Data-Driven Design | UX Magazine." UX Magazine | Defining and

Informing the Complex Field of User Experience (UX). Last modified December 10, 2013. https://uxmag.com/articles/unlocking-the-power-of-data-driven-design.

Schutt, Cathy O'Neil. Rachel. *Doing Data Science.* Sebastopol, CA: O'Reilly Media, Inc, 2013.

Siegel, Eric. *Predictive Analytics The Power to Predict Who Will Click, Buy, Lie, or Die.* Hoboken, New Jersey: John Wiley & Sons, Inc, 2013.

University of California, Berkely. "Data Analysis Toolkits." UC Berkeley Seismology Lab. Accessed January 29, 2017. http://seismo.berkeley.edu/~kirchner/eps_120/EPSToolkits.htm.

Zumel, Nina, and John Mount. *Practical Data Science with R.* Shelter Island, NY: Manning Publications, 2014.

Chapter 6
Design Practices for Data Use

Now that we understand the different types of data that are available, we can start talking about the many ways to use data in design decisions. If we look to other industries – web design, marketing, etc. – we see data used widely to make informed, effective design decisions. Marketing uses data like Nielsen ratings to measure many items such as viewership of a commercial, product packaging, and sales effectiveness of particular items, among others. The data collected directly affects the way marketers create commercials, produce eye-catching packages, and set up stores for better sales. Marketers also use Google Analytics to track things like how many people visit a site, or how many people started a transaction and then actually bought something. Web designers use this data to optimize the user experience and interface design to satisfy the target audience. A bad user experience on a website can taint even the best product for a lot of people. Marketers and web designers take great care in using data to make sure that both the content being delivered and the interface in which it is delivered are the best they can be. These are not arbitrary decisions; they are based on carefully collected and analyzed data.

As L&D practitioners we should look to these industries for guidance and avoid the mistakes they have already made. L&D is closely related to both of these industries: our interventions look and feel like web pages and can use the same design principles. Also, our content is much like marketing, for although we are not necessarily trying to sell things, we are trying to get the people we support involved in the content.

Why Design with Data?

By this point you may be wondering, how do I get started with data-driven design? Where does data-driven design fit into my design/development cycle? Shai Wininger gives good tips on designing for and with data. He calls it fact-driven design, but the principles are the same. Here we will focus on the five steps to "fact-driven design heaven" that Shai lays out:

1. "Define business objectives as clear, measurable key performance indicators." Does this sound familiar? When designing learning content we should be figuring out how the content relates to our business. We are looking at what behavior we are trying to change.
2. "Come up with a hypothesis that aims to improve at least one of the KPIs." So now that we know what we are trying to improve, we need to figure out, how are we going to do that?
3. "Build your changes." In our case we need to build our prototype to collect data about the design.
4. "Test [the design]." While we might not be doing traditional A/B Testing, we do need to test designs. Testing is critical to producing an end result that gets us the data we need.
5. "Repeat from step 2 (forever . . .)" is the final step. We commonly refer to this as the feedback loop. We shouldn't simply deploy a solution and forget about it. The feedback loop is critical to deploying solutions that are meaningful to our end learner base.

In the next section we'll go through the five steps as Shai has laid them out, but using L&D scenarios.

Define business objectives and performance indicators
What am I trying to change?

As learning professionals we should always have in mind a specific behavior that we are trying to change. When we are thinking about creating an intervention, the most critical step is figuring out what needs changing. And the more we tie ourselves to the bottom line, the more impact we will have on the business. We find these critical objectives by working with the other departments in our organization. For example, if the sales department is struggling with certain types of sales we should define what successful behavior change looks like for the sales department. We need to ask questions such as, What are the key indicators that make a salesperson successful in this type of sale? What is the demographic information of the successful salespeople? Is there a common thread that can be used to form a basis of knowledge each salesperson needs? Asking questions such as these will help us figure out the type of intervention needed for the salespeople. Once we have deployed a solution, we need to measure if the intervention was effective.

When we think about data, the question becomes, how do I measure that change? Collecting the data to measure behavior change accurately is the holy grail of the L&D profession. It moves us beyond return on investment (ROI) and straight to the bottom line. If the right data is used to make the design effective, we can show the real benefit to the business bottom line. It all starts with asking the right questions. By asking the right questions we can figure out what data we need to collect and how we do it.

Create a Hypothesis about a KPI
How can I test impact on the behavior I am trying to change?

We are now ready to start experimenting. First, we need to start thinking about the data we need to collect to prove that we are changing a behavior. As stated earlier, we need to work with subject matter experts (SMEs) and managers to get a clear picture of what they think the learners need. From the interviews and information collected we can start to make a hypothesis of the problem we are trying to solve. To start, what do we mean by a hypothesis? We can define it as "a supposition or proposed explanation made on the basis of limited evidence as a starting point for further investigation."[1] In other words, we are stating what we think will happen as a result of the intervention that we are providing to the learners. A valid hypothesis must be testable and refutable. We have to be able to test the outcome, and we must be able to prove that the hypothesis is potentially wrong. In learning, it is probably safe to say that being able to prove a hypothesis wrong is pretty much a given. We are not typically building interventions for things we are completely sure will work. We are trying to find what it is that makes something testable. At the same time, the refutability is useful in that it means that the hypothesis must be arguable and lead us to evidence we can validate or invalidate. Basically, we need something that we can document and confirm or deny with evidence. We need observational ability, to gather and measure the evidence. We also need to be able to control influencing factors. For example, in sales, a major new product release coinciding with the end of sales training would add another variable (which is not isolatable) to the equation.

To look at an example of a hypothesis, and a process we might use to prove or disprove the hypothesis, let's continue with our earlier example of sales training. We might form a hypothesis that if salespeople are more knowledgeable about the product, their sales will increase. To prove this hypothesis we would need to have sales data prior to the intervention and sales data after the intervention to perform a comparison. We would also want to look at data collected from the intervention to see what took place while taking the training. It is important to make sure the hypothesis is something that can be proven. The hypothesis we use in this example can be proven using the pre and post sales data along with data collected from the intervention. We can tell if the intervention training on the product actually helped improve the sales numbers.

What does it look like when we create a hypothesis that does not meet our criteria? The hypothesis might be rendered invalid by circumstances not directly related to the hypothesis. We might make a perfectly valid hypothesis, but extenuating circumstances will cause us to be unable to prove or deny the hypothesis. To go back to the example above, let's say we have built an intervention that educates the salespeople on the product line. We check our data and see that sales improve, but we find out that the sales team also started group collaboration sessions focused on the product line at the same time. What actually led to the increased sales? It could have been the intervention that we deployed or it could have been the collaboration sessions. We have no way to isolate what affected the outcome.

With a hypothesis that we can prove, we can formulate the plan to build our content to meet the end needs of the learners, questions can be formulated, and the content prototypes can be built. Testing the hypothesis is going to show us whether our intervention is actually providing the behavior change we intend. We might find, as we look through the data, that our intervention meets all or part of the need expressed by the hypothesis. Based on these outcomes, we can develop our plan going forward. The results from the data collected should show us where our intervention is deficient and where it is working well. From there we can make the necessary changes to "fill the gaps" that currently exist. We can make decisions on content and interface based on the data and feedback that we collect. Often, we might see opportunities to improve both content and presentation. We might have great content, but the path to access the content is cumbersome, and if the path is too hard, we are likely to lose the learners' attention. We might have the best user interface, one that is easy to understand, but our content lacks the information that the learners need.

The challenge of solving these problems shows the importance of working with both qualitative and quantitative data while testing the hypothesis. For example, let's say we have an intervention that uses a process-based intervention to expose content. A learner must follow the correct process path to get all of the content and complete the intervention. We test with a cross section of learners and see that a majority are not exposing all of the content. We might not have noticed that the path to the content is hard for the learners because we did initial testing with SMEs who understood the process. For a new or inexperienced learner, however, it doesn't make sense. We might not know this unless we talk to learners from across the demographic groups. We might see that learners are not accessing the content, but to make informed decisions about corrections, we need to understand why and what their background is. When we collect data for the purpose of proving or disproving a hypothesis and making informed changes, the answer might not be readily apparent. We might need to do a certain amount of digging into the data and talking with learners. At this stage we would be asking not just what data we need to collect from our learning products, but what we might need from outside our department. What data are the end user organizations collecting that will show us how our learning intervention is affecting the learners? In most instances, outside information is going to be critical when trying to show real behavior change.

Data might include sales data, safety data, or performance data collected for individual learners. If we can tie the data we collect to the data collected by the organization we can start to see where we are making improvements. Talking with the end user organizations will help us predict what data we need, which in turn will allow us to come up with better solutions for improving the behavior we are trying to change. Gone are the days of the L&D department sitting in a silo. Working with other departments adds value to what we do.

Build Your Change
What can be done to target the identified behavior?

Your hypothesis should be designed to test a particular behavior. A warning: if you try to test a particular behavior when interface and content changes are being made simultaneously, you will end up with mixed findings. Make each change on its own, and test it in order to identify triggers. Perhaps you've moved a button and added a paragraph, and subsequent testing shows a change in the desired behavior. Was it the button move or the added paragraph that triggered the change? Was it both? How do you know?

Interface Design

A rule of thumb when looking at interface design is that there is not one "right" way to design an interface. Each project is going to be different based on the audience.

Testing early and often with a cross section of your audience is what you need to prove that a design is effective.

Finding a cross section of the audience is critical to using data successfully in your design. If you limit testing to one or two learners of a certain demographic, you will end up with a design that tends to align itself with those learners' biases. If you then deploy to others outside of that demographic, you might not deliver an intervention that is as effective as it could be. The data needs to provide a sufficient cross section against which you can make decisions and hit a good middle ground with all end learners.

Fortunately, we have many available methods to collect the data for the interface design.

Before building out a full interface, we can test designs with prototypes. Prototypes can be made quickly and easily with paper or wireframes. Paper prototypes allow us to use learner observation. Or we can use xAPI in wireframe prototypes to see what people are interacting with and what path they take through a particular set of screens. We can then follow up by interviewing learners to gain insight into why they clicked on certain things. Of course, the point of a prototype is to iterate quickly. Depending on your resources, you may want to wait to integrate xAPI until the final product. If that's the case, learner observation can be done with wireframes as well.

Our goal for the interface is for it to disappear into the background of our intervention as much as possible. We want our learners to interact with the content, not be distracted by the interface. The greatest content will have no traction if the delivery method (the interface) is terrible. It also works in the other direction. And yet if we focus too much on the interface and forget about content, we will end up with an intervention that does not work. Content and interface go hand in hand when creating an effective design.

Content

Ultimately, content matters more to the success of our

intervention than the interface. The content is what can change the behavior. Fortunately, we can test the content, just as we do with the interface. And it is worth repeating: we want the interface to become as invisible as possible, so that people are immersed in the content. We want our learners to be interacting with the content as they move through an intervention.

In the testing stage, it is not necessary to have the final content. Finalized content will come later, almost at the end of the design process. Fortunately, though, we can include finalized content in the prototypes as it becomes available. When evaluating the content, we ask questions similar to those we asked when evaluating the interface design, such as:

- What are learners interacting with? Are they interacting with the content they need to be focusing on?
- How are different demographics operating as learners work through the content?
- Is the deployment of this content changing the behavior we want to change?

This last question is the most critical. It points us to the bottom line of the intervention that we are creating.

The initial content should come from the SMEs providing the outline. From the outline we can create a content map, and the content map will provide overall organization of the content for delivery to learners. In the early stages it can be helpful to interview end learners for some guidance toward content creation. We can ask simple questions such as:

- What content do you think you need to gain this knowledge?
- How will this knowledge help you in your role?
- What are your day-to-day tasks?
- What information would help you in those tasks?

Asking these types of questions will help determine how content should be delivered to be effective for the learner base. In many cases we find that a combination of content delivery methods will work. For example, we might find that an online module will help deliver the knowledge of a concept but will not help with day-to-day tasks. To help with the latter, a simple job aid might also be needed. We know this from qualitative data we have collected through interviews.

If interviewing the SME, we can ask simple questions such as:

- What information helped you in your journey from novice to expert?
- Where do you point people when they ask you questions?
- What best practice advice would you give to novices?

Using the personal experience of the experts will help frame the content for the end learners. SMEs may suggest a form they think is right for delivery. However, after interviewing SMEs and end learners you may find better methods of delivery. The decision should not be arbitrary; it should be based on the data collected from those learners.

The data collection does not end here while designing. The quantitative and qualitative data you collect in these early stages will provide you with the tools to make a more effective end result. You won't be guessing what will work for your learners; you will have a direction based on feedback from the learners. And remember: not every piece of feedback from every learner is going to be used. The data collected is subject to a certain amount of processing as we find the patterns that emerge across a majority of the learners. If we try to use every piece of learner feedback, we are likely to build something that will not be particularly useful to any of the learners.

After building the content, we start testing the delivery methods.

Test the Design
How do you test a design's effectiveness?

This is a stage that will be very iterative. As data starts to come in, you might change elements in the interface and in the content. One word of warning: do not make significant changes from a small sample size. If you do not have a diverse set of data, results can skew, causing you to make unnecessary changes. At this stage, you can simply run the material updated from the data collected against the original to make sure the changes you are making are having a positive effect on the end-learner (A/B Testing).

Once through the initial design and builds of the content, we can test the two together for a combined set of data. At this point we also have a great opportunity to test the delivery methods we have chosen for this intervention. If we have created an online module, are we getting the knowledge transfer we want to get? If not, do we see where we could potentially make changes? If we are using a job aid, we can ask, are people actually using it? If yes, is it helpful? Getting feedback such as this during testing will lead to a much more successful deployment of the intervention. Furthermore, if we have done our early rounds of feedback and prototyping effectively, then we won't have wide-scale changes to make at this point, only tweaks and minor updates.

If you find yourself making wide-scale changes – for example, in delivery methodology or in large portions of the content – then you should revisit your prototyping methods and results. There is a good chance that the demographics tested were not representative or that the data was misread or misrepresented in the output. Such things happen occasionally but should be the exception rather than the rule.

Repeat from Step 2 (forever . . .)
What should a feedback loop include?

Revisiting designs based on the collected data is critical to the continued success of an intervention. When a round of iterations is finished, don't stop; create a schedule for the next review of that design. Depending on the number of people this design serves and how critical it is to your work, you may want to do this in a day, a week, or a few months. In this review you will review the data supporting the feedback loop you have created and decide whether another iteration of the design would be beneficial. You shouldn't make design changes for the sake of changing, but you should continually review content according to data that you collect.

The feedback loop is the holy grail of many industries, such as marketing and web design, and L&D professionals should hold it dear as well. How many times do we deploy a solution and never return to it? We move on to the next thing until it is time to make a content update or process changes requiring an update. Why is this? Do we lack the right data to see what people are accessing? Are we not looking at the data in the context of design? Probably a combination of many factors is causing this situation.

If we design with data collection in mind, then we no longer have an excuse. As we collect the data from our courses, job aids, modules, etc., we can see where there may be issues in the content that need to be addressed. We should want this feedback; we can't look at it as a failure if something is not being used as we intended. We have the opportunity to make informed changes to the interface and content to make them work better. (See the sidebar for examples of what we can look for in the data to help us make changes.) When we use the data we have collected we are no longer making arbitrary changes. Our changes are based not on opinions but on the facts provided by the data. We are making informed decisions about changes that need to be made.

Ultimately, there is no magic equation for designing with data in mind. Each project will be a little bit different, and the targets will be unique to the organization. In some cases, different organizations need different data from the same course. Forethought and leg work are needed at the beginning to flesh out the requirements for data capture. In many cases, we may need to work with other departments in our organizations to get the end result data we need to prove our results.

The intervention data is not the end-all-be-all of the data needed to prove behavior change. We might need data from other departments within the company. The information we use to show behavior change is not in the LMS or the LRS, or even necessarily controlled by the L&D department. It will likely come from overall organizational data. The sales team, the safety team, the marketing team, and many others hold the data that we need to form the full feedback loop. (See the sidebar for an example of data we might need from another department.) We will need to work with these departments to build the story and show that we achieved the desired result.

We affect the bottom line of the company. We can strive to prove that we increased sales. We can prove that we helped improve safety with the compliance training that we gave. People were able to access the content they needed, when they needed help with a task. This is our true goal: making significant improvements in the day-to-day jobs of the people we support.

Sidebar
Patterns in Data

There will be many ways that we can examine data to learn about content. One of the main things we can look for is a pattern in the data collected. Patterns help us figure out how the content is being used. For example, perhaps we have added a video to a module. If we are tracking people's interactions with the video we might see that a large number of them are pausing the video at the same point. Why are they doing that? It could be a point of confusion, it could be to get more information on a topic, it could be that we have lost them and they are moving on to another topic (which we should be able to find out from our data). The pattern provides us with feedback that we can explore further. We can interview a cross section of learners to find out why they paused at that point. Depending on what we find out, we can adjust the content to make it fit the need better.

In another example we might have a page with a click interaction that allows learners to reveal content as they see fit. We notice in our data analysis that content we deemed important for novice learners is not being accessed by anyone regardless of background. The content is reflected directly in a question in our assessment, and the question is answered wrong a majority of the time by the novice learners. Why? There could be many reasons for this behavior. Maybe our design distracts from the click that will reveal the content. Maybe we have not stressed the importance of this piece of content to the novice learner. We can interview learners to find why they skipped over the content. We can then make adjustments to the content based on analysis of the data we collected and the interviews we conducted. There are many ways the feedback loop becomes important to the continued analysis of deployed solutions. We hope that these examples illustrate ways that you can use data to make informed adjustments to content, ensuring that the needs of the learner base are met.

Sidebar
Data-Driven Design Example

Let's look at a practical example of data-driven design. We have a sales team made up of a mixed group of new and experienced salespeople. The sales department sees that some of the sales staff struggle with a certain type of sale. The sales department comes to the L&D department to help create a training intervention to bring up the level of the staff for these sales.

The sales department uses Salesforce to track sales and has lots of data showing the different sales types and where the sales staff is struggling. Working with SMEs from the sales department we develop content for the training. The content creation includes asking veteran members what helped them move from a novice to an expert on the products. We decide to run an online module to train the staff on the products being sold.

We interview a cross section of the sales staff to gain knowledge on the demographics. The demographics range from staff that has been with the company for many years to new staff members. Looking at the cross section we set up the module to contain chunks of content that can be accessed by the staff. Seasoned veterans can access needed content while the new members can access all content within the module. Data is collected from each interaction with content to see how the staff interacts with the module.

During testing we see the how the levels of expertise interact with the content. By analyzing the interaction data we can see how the different salespeople view their knowledge. We also give each learner a post-module knowledge check. We can then look at the interaction data and compare it to the post-module assessment. Does this comparison show whether they are better at the type of sales we are trying to improve? Not necessarily. Just because someone interacted with content doesn't mean their sales will improve. At least, it's not something we can prove just from the interaction data. We can see if they can answer the test questions correctly. We can see if our content helped them answer the questions based on the interaction points and any wrong answers that were posted. We can even introduce a pre-test to see if knowledge was gained. But we still won't know if we improved the sales and changed the behavior. We would need to work with the sales department to get actual real world data from the sales being made.

We can look at sales data pre-intervention and sales data post-intervention to see if we improved the behavior of the sales staff. We can see what demographic was the biggest beneficiary of the training. We can also look at how individual learners accessed our module and how their sales were affected. Depending on the results, we can offer further training or, if needed, ensure that all necessary content was viewed in the module. By working with other departments to mine the data that they collect, we can see whether the approach we are taking is making a dent in the bottom line of the company.

Designing for/with xAPI

When designing for xAPI, we need to keep certain things at the forefront of our decision-making. First and foremost is deciding what we need to track. While xAPI affords us the opportunity to track almost everything, this may not be the best choice. If we track everything we will likely end up with data that is not useful, and we will find ourselves wading through the data to find something that is useful. More data is not always a good thing. Therefore as we start to design our intervention we need to ask, "What is going to give me data that shows this is working?"

Earlier we talked about design and how to create effective designs. Now that we are honing the design we can start to tag the elements in it that we want to track. We are looking at the path that someone took through the content. Given the path they took, did they find the information there useful? How did the qualitative data they provided (background, experience, goals, etc.) affect the path they took?

We can use xAPI to find the qualitative data we are looking for to validate what we have done. The great thing about using xAPI is that we can implement it early in the design process. We can use the xAPI data as the basis for what we ask people in interviews or follow-ups. As we add xAPI capabilities to our interventions we start to see patterns emerging. If someone has a particular experience level he or she may interact with the content and interface in a certain way. For example, we might be explaining a concept and then offering the process of using that concept. An experienced person might skip over the explanation because they already know what the concept is, and they just need to know the "how." By adding xAPI early in the design process we can start to understand what items we need to track.

In the beginning you will probably collect too much data and try to track too many things – and this is OK in the early stages. This is why we prototype and do the early learner testing, because then we can home in on the critical items with a small amount of data. Later when we are deploying and working with large amounts of data we will have the critical statements that we need to see. Once we have figured out the critical components to track, there are some other key decisions to make. We need to come up with a data strategy for xAPI data describing a specific set of interactions. This is often called a profile in the xAPI community. The profile outlines the commonality among the statements throughout the interventions that we are creating. The key pieces are the verb, the activity type, any extensions being used, and how all of it operates for an experience. Some experiences already have communities of practice that are prescribing profiles for the experiences. (See the links at the end of the chapter to see those communities of practice.) If there is no existing profile for your application in the community, it is a good idea to build a profile for your organization. If nothing else, it will provide commonality for statements within your own organization.

If the statement language is not common within your organization it will make analysis across different interventions nearly impossible. For example, we might have a link in a module to an external document, and we want to know when someone accesses the document from the module. When building the statement there are several verbs that can be used to express this action. We can say that someone "opened" the document. We can say that someone "clicked" the link to open the document. We can say that someone "interacted" with the link on the page to open the document. We now have three different verbs describing the same interaction. If we have three developers using these three different verbs it will be difficult to get good analytics from the collected data. If we have defined a data strategy for the organization, however, we will have consistent data from all xAPI enabled interactions. If we use the verb "opened" we can filter the data quite easily to see how many opens we have, who opened, and then expand to see the path taken before or after the opens.

What we have just described is called data modeling. Data modeling is defined as "the act of exploring data-oriented structures." In data modeling, data attributes (verbs, extensions, activities, activity types) are assigned to entity types (buttons, links, content interactions) to create the model. The data model provides the consistency, which is key for usable data.

Custom vs. Rapid eLearning Development

We have one issue when creating our xAPI-enabled interventions. Our choice of development method can limit what we are able to do from an xAPI standpoint. Custom-developed solutions such as an HTML-based module allow for an open model. In other words, we can create almost anything we want. The profile we have implemented for statements is the only thing that binds us. Therefore when working with custom-built solutions it is critically important to have developed profiles.

When we use rapid development tools, the process tends to be different. With rapid development tools we are often prescribed the verbs, activity types, activity identification, and the extensions. These are limited out of the box. In most cases there is a small number of verbs automatically assigned by the tool, and interactions will be limited to those that are in the tool. For example, most tools will track only what pages or slides are visited using the verb "experienced." Interactions within a page or slide cannot be recorded without customization or work-arounds in the tool. The tool will limit the verbs that are available in the output. If you have the ability to customize, most tools will allow for JavaScript to be launched through some action. This can be used to customize the tool and extend its capabilities.

The xAPI Quarterly has a set of living documents that cover the capabilities and best practices for a number of rapid tools on the market. (See the links section at the end of this chapter to review those documents for your tool of choice.) It is still up to you to decide what you will track with the rapid tools and to make sure that your organization is using them consistently for data tracking. The data modeling principles should continue to be applied to make sure each developer is working in a consistent method. If not, the data will be hard to analyze, even if there is consistent output.

There is no magic formula for data-driven design. Testing with learners to gather qualitative data and setting up xAPI on the content as early as possible to gather quantitative data will help guide you in the pursuit of meaningful data. At the same time, you will have to keep in mind all the questions that need to be answered to demonstrate behavior change and how the bottom line of the business is affected.

Reference

Shai Wininger, Fiverr.com "Fact-Driven Design: Optimize Your Optimizations" [sponsored content], Wired.com, October 2013. http://www.wired.com/insights/2013/10/fact-driven-design-optimize-your-optimizations/

Ambler, Scott. "Data Modeling 101". Accessed January 26,2017 http://www.agiledata.org/essays/dataModeling101.html

Chapter 7

Content Strategy Overview

Data is rife with potential, but is it the potential to create useful information or the potential to create total chaos? The answer hinges on whether we attach some content strategy to our data projects. The good news is that content strategy is not new: there is already a strong body of resources on content strategy for the web, and that's a good starting point if we want to crib some notes for the area of learning data.

For the area of learning, we propose looking at content strategy from two angles: first, to look at our content strategy for courses; then, to look at our content strategy for our data. Fortunately, both of these connect to the same root questions – the questions that form the basis of all our work in learning.

It all comes down to goals:

- Goals in the organizational context – These are the fundamental instructional design questions that delve into why this learning intervention exists in the first place. (Horton; Piskurich)
- Goals with respect to learners' gaps – Knowing the kinds of problems we are trying to solve in the area of learning is key to knowing what course content and what data actually matter. (Dirksen)
- Goals with respect to the learner's destination, or "learning objectives" – These are how we are defining success for each learner, and success for the course.

It is perhaps most accurate to say that content strategy ultimately comes down to how our goals intersect with reality.

Align

Alignment is the first thing we must address when we're working with content strategy, and it's a key element that we'll touch on again and again. When we keep key players and stakeholders aligned throughout the life cycle of developing and maintaining content strategy, we limit the odds that we'll encounter painful surprises or miss out on critical details.

When we talk about alignment, we're talking mostly about a human issue, but not exclusively so. Agreements are reached by people, but processes and technology are also factors. When we are engaged in learning content strategy we need to make sure that we address stakeholder alignment in the context of:

- Organizational goals
- Instructional design / L&D goals
- Existing courseware
- Data availability and interoperability

For any given course or module this means that we need to identify the key stakeholders and key players and then reach agreement on some basic questions, such as:

- What's the point of the course; what needs is it meeting and for whom?
- How do we define/measure success?
- What are the key elements/learning objects/ learning paths of the course?
- What courseware or other tools are we using; how will those choices affect design and data availability?

Ideally these are the sorts of questions that the instructional design process worked through early on, but if they were not, or if the course is old enough that they haven't been discussed in a while, then this is a good time to make sure those details get codified. After all, they're going to be important in the audit phase, because by then, if you haven't defined clearly what you're doing, it will be hard to know what you need to do to get it done.

When we're looking at designing for data, we need to add another layer to the learning content strategy. Just as we need to have alignment on what the expectations are for a given course, we need alignment regarding the data. As always, this starts with identifying the key stakeholders and players. If we know what the point of the course is, we're on our way to building some consensus and shared understanding about our data objectives:

- What should we measure?
    - What do we want to learn about the course? (Did it work? What parts? For whom?)
    - What do we want to learn about our users? (Ticking boxes? Career development?)
- What technical, ethical, or regulatory issues might impact our data objectives?

Once we have clearly delineated our goals for the course and our goals for the course data, we will need to take a good look at the reality of what we have (Audit), and how we can reach our goals (Strategy).

Audit

When we perform a content audit, in the context of our content strategy, ultimately we're looking to determine how well our content meets our information goals. In practice this means we audit our content in two spheres: courses and data. If we've achieved at least some preliminary alignment with respect to our course goals and our data needs, we have a solid basis from which to begin our audit.

As we look through the elements of each course – interfaces, content objects, activities – we can assess how they fit with the course goals and how best to measure whether they are serving the purpose for which they were intended. This means looking at them in the context of instructional design: Is the content covering the bases we intended? Is it falling short in some areas? Is it going outside the relevant scope in others? We must bring care and attention to the audit but also an awareness that it is a first pass in an iterative process.

Our audit may be ID or pedagogically focused, but we also want to take a look at the course from a UI perspective. We want to really understand how users interact with the course interface. This is where paper prototypes or wireframes (as discussed in Chapter 6) will come in handy, because looking at the physical structure of the course allows us to understand how users interact with the materials, which in turn gives a clearer picture of what data will be available.

In Chapters 4 and 5, we looked at quantitative and qualitative data; in an audit we will put those concepts to work, so let's look at what kinds of data we are able to get.

In terms of quantitative data, we might have everything from basic information about number of object views and assessment scores to time spent on site. We may have the ability to get more interesting information such as interactions with videos, or patterns of navigation, or similar details that will allow us to establish correlation between various activity patterns and performance. We will also have the opportunity to collect potentially pointless data – we probably don't need to assess every click or keystroke, but what data actually matters will vary by course. Auditing tells us what we have; when we get to strategy, we determine what we need.

Similarly, we will want to look at possible qualitative data from our courses. Depending on the course design, the volume could be very extensive or quite minimal. Qualitative data is often of very high value, but it can also be more demanding to work with in terms of time and effort. At the audit stage we simply want to notice what elements of the course might generate qualitative data and what form that data might take.

In the auditing process, we need to remember that in the world of xAPI, learning data can come from across a variety of channels. (CAI) If learning is happening both within and outside the LMS we need to keep all our learning arenas and all related data sources in mind. The data from courseware and the data from other sources will differ because of potential differences in user activities and the data they generate. When we are working with data generated by different courseware, even the available xAPI data will vary to some degree for similar content across different platforms.

When we know what data we can get, it's time to pare away the data that is less likely to be useful and to think about how to combine potential data to make it more useful. In short, it's time to look at strategy.

Strategy

As we found with Alignment and Audit, we find that our Strategy for our data is determined by the nature and strategy behind the course (or other learning activity). Strategy will also be driven by the data available. Ultimately, if we do things right, over time our strategy for the course will also be driven by what is learned from our data; this may happen because we are using feedback from our data to improve course content, or perhaps we determine that small changes to the course mechanics improve the data available to meet our analysis needs. Working with learning data is an iterative process, and by taking careful steps in content strategy we can make that iteration more effective and efficient, ultimately benefiting our learners and our organizations.

We should look to the course and data goals from the alignment phase as the foundation of our data strategy; the specific details that we discover within the audit allow us to develop the smaller goals within our larger goals. In other words, if alignment helps set the strategy, the audit helps determine the tactics to meet the strategic goals.

For example, how might course content impact data content strategy? Let's imagine we have a course that is intended to increase certain aspects of sales capability for a new product. As part of that course, users upload videos illustrating a concept or action which will be critiqued by their peers; they, in turn, are expected to critique others' videos. In order to understand what data to collect, we need to understand the content and what impact this is expected to have on the overall course strategy. And we need to create strategic data goals, asking what data will give us the insights we need, and how we can compensate if some preferred data is not available.

In situations like this, we often need some amount of qualitative data with respect to efficacy and best practices. Fortunately, we know, through our audit, how the course mechanics work and what available data can help us determine the combinations of quantitative data that will meet our needs, and also when we need to work with more cumbersome, but content-rich, qualitative data to answer our strategic needs.

While it may be the nature of course content that drives our data strategy, sometimes it is our data that can drive improvements in course content strategy. For example, in our early work with data from a course, we might examine data on time spent on course objects, object revisits, and the quality of conversation/submissions associated with various objects. Perhaps from this data we discover that there is a valid correlation of interaction with certain objects and future on-the-job performance. This is an opportunity for highly informed course improvement strategies.

Data content strategy, with its interplay of course mechanics and course goals with data availability and data goals, is a key stepping stone to the creation of a valid feedback loop. Let's see what this looks like in real life.

Profiles

You may recall reading about profiles for xAPI in Chapter 2; in fact they are pretty closely tied to content strategy. The understanding of data that we develop through this process is central to developing profiles effectively.

Let's say that the Acme Anvil corporation wants to deliver training to their sales force as they prepare for the launch of their new Titanium Anvil.

They have some specific goals for the training: they want sales reps to be able to explain, effectively and articulately:

- Product features and benefits
- Comparison to other models in the product line
- Installation requirements
- Skills required for use of the new product

And at the end of the day, they want to know if the training worked, in terms of providing the right resources – resources that are effective enough to make a difference and engaging enough that people will make use of them. In other words, they're looking at questions of course performance and individual performance.

If we want to collect data from this course, we need to look at the course objectives, the information objectives, and the course design in order to design xAPI statements that will get us the data we really need. While we might not design things perfectly on the first pass, we should try to get it right to the extent that we can, because we're collecting data in real time, and we don't want to miss opportunities.

We've already touched on the basic components of xAPI profiles in Chapter 2, and it's fairly simple to find online resources that provide profiles for common actions in courses. Or, if you're using specific courseware, you may find that there are predefined statements. But what we need to do is create a plan for the specific data we want from our course, for the questions we want answered. Generic statements are a good place to start getting a handle on xAPI, but we need to work in the context of our actual design, mechanics, learning goals, and data goals.

We suggest, as a first step, looking at any wireframes or storyboarding that's been done or any course prototypes. This gives us a good look at the kinds of interactions a user is likely to have with a course. To some degree this is not unlike looking at usability for websites – what we are thinking about is what people are likely to do and how they're likely to do it (Krug). From there we determine what is meaningful for different kinds of analysis.

It's helpful to start with some tables or a spreadsheet where we can note possible actions and their associated objects – things like "Spock logged in to Course A, Level 1" or "McCoy pressed pause on Video B at timestamp 12:34." Starting out with a list of the possible verbs we'll use, as well as a list of the relevant objects and their respective activity types, puts us on a good footing for planning our profiles.

It's also useful, for future reference, to create a spreadsheet for course actions and interactions, listing the appropriate verbs, formal definitions and the IRI for each verb. Another spreadsheet could be used for the objects and activity types associated with those objects. From there it's fairly straightforward to determine the various actions users will take within each element of the course and lay out some basic statements we want to collect.

At this point we will also want to think about not just the actions people take within the course but also what we need to know to perform meaningful analysis. We want to take a good look at context, and for all potentially relevant interactions, we will want to look at what data is needed to provide meaningful analysis. This could include user metadata, results from an action taken, or the additional context of descriptions.

For our hypothetical sales course, the Acme Anvil Company wants to understand whether the course is useful, and they also want to understand how users engage with the course. Are all the activities and learning objects necessary? Are some more valuable than others? Are any of them confusing? Do the answers differ for different user personae? So we start to consider possible course actions and resultant data:

Interaction	Verb	Context	Object	Result	Extensions
Played Demo Video					
Paused Demo Video					
Commented on Demo Video				Response: string or answer choice Success: true or false	
Assessment question answered	http://adlnet.gov/expapi/verbs/answered	Parent: Quiz ID	http://adlnet.gov/expapi/activities/question	Response: string or answer choice Success: true or false	
Assessment completed	http://adlnet.gov/expapi/verbs/completed	Parent: Lesson ID	http://adlnet.gov/expapi/activities/assessment	Result: Score	

Back to the Future

Content strategy tends to be something that evolves and develops over time; it's not a static final product. Even so, good strategic planning needs to be well documented – it's a way of future-proofing your work – because three months after you set things up, chances are high that you'll remember very little of the decisions that got you to where you are. If you want to improve your data and analytics processes continuously, it helps to have a well-defined benchmark of the current state of your learning data. As part of any data project, it is important to keep records of data plans and definitions, including details on the ownership and documentation of life cycles and future goals, in order to keep your data collection relevant and useful. This brings us into the arena of Data Stewardship, which is one of the not-glamorous-but-essential elements for successful data wrangling. We'll dig into that important topic in more detail in Chapter 10, but for now, we'll assume that you've worked through some content strategy, you're starting to get some valuable data, and you want to start turning that data into information, so it's time to think about analysis.

References

Advanced Distributed Learning. "Experience XAPI Vocabulary Primer · Experience XAPI Vocabulary Primer." Adl (@adl) on GitBook · GitBook. Accessed January 26, 2017. https://adl. gitbooks.io/experience-xapi-vocabulary-primer/content/.

Advanced Distributed Learning. "Companion Specification for XAPI Vocabularies." Adl (@adl) on GitBook · GitBook. Accessed January 26, 2017. https://adl.gitbooks.io/ companion-specification-for-xapi-vocabularies/content/.

Bowe, Megan. "The Future of Learning Content Strategy." Making Better. Last modified January 30, 2014. makingbetter.us/2014/01/ the-future-of-learning-content-strategy-presentation-from-astdtk14

Clark, Donald. "Big Data: Ten Level Taxonomy in Learning." Donald Clark Plan B. Accessed January 26, 2017. http://donaldclarkplanb.blogspot.co.uk/2013/11/ big-data-ten-level-taxonomy-in-learning.html.

Dirksen, Julie. *Design for How People Learn.* Berkeley, CA: New Riders, 2011.

Fleisher, Craig S., and Babette E. Bensoussan. *Business and Competitive Analysis: Effective Application of New and Classic Methods.* Upper Saddle River, NJ: Financial Times Press, 2007.

Foreman, John W. *Data Smart: Using Data Science to Transform Information into Insight.* Indianapolis: John Wiley & Sons, 2014.

Halvorson, Kristina, and Melissa Rach. *Content Strategy for the Web.* Berkeley: New Riders, 2012.

Liebowitz, Jay. *Strategic Intelligence: Business Intelligence, Competitive Intelligence, and Knowledge Management.* Boca Raton: Auerbach Publications, 2006.

Mayring, Philipp. "Qualitative Content Analysis." Forum Qualitative Sozialforschung / Forum: Qualitative Social Research. Last modified June 2000. http://www.qualitative-research.net/index.php/fqs/article/viewArticle/1089/2385.

Shea, Peter, and Temi Bidjerano. "Community of inquiry as a theoretical framework to foster "epistemic engagement" and "cognitive presence" in online education." *Computers & Education* 52, no. 3 (2009), 543-553. doi:10.1016/j.compedu.2008.10.007.

Siemens, George, and Ryan S. Baker. "Learning Analytics and Educational Data Mining: Towards Communication and Collaboration." Worcester Polytechnic Institute. Accessed January 26, 2017. http://users.wpi.edu/~rsbaker/LAKs%20reformatting%20v2.pdf.

Chapter 8

Analysis 101

No matter how good your data collection plan is, no matter what efforts you've put into ensuring that you have useful, good-quality data, you won't know what your data can tell you until you start analyzing.

And although we all like to imagine the results of our data collection efforts looking as clean as a pristine dashboard – optimally designed with clear and motivating visualizations – that's not where we start. First, we roll up our sleeves and get to know our data. If we don't get our hands dirty, we won't know what the data means when it's displayed in a dashboard, and we won't know if our dashboard elements even make sense.

We might assume that data collected from courses and carefully planned xAPI statements would be both orderly and complete. What could possibly go wrong?

Quite a lot, as it turns out – but if we don't take time to look things over, we might not even know that there are problems.

The problem could be something simple – users ending up with multiple signups (individual users signing up with more than one account), or user IDs being based on actual names, which poses obvious problems if we have multiple users with the same name. Or it could be a more complicated situation – we spot inconsistencies, or the numbers seem unrealistic. In a perfect world, none of these problems would happen, but in the real world they happen all the time. Through data exploration, we can find issues and address them before they lead us to a flawed analysis.

Data exploration

Data is messy – there's no getting around it. Even if we export data to a csv (comma separated values) file, it doesn't look very useful:

```
●  ●  ●                          download (12).csv
id,object-id,object-name,parent-id,parent-name,verb-id
3dd108ac-7a41-4d7b-a01f-b459cfe29e9c,http://beta.curatr3.com/courses/xapi/home#object/
11935,"Building a Learning Record Store",null,null,http://adlnet.gov/expapi/verbs/completed
b531a370-ab1e-49c9-9b7d-5c49f4256c9e,http://beta.curatr3.com/courses/xapi/home#object/11934/
comment/60346,"comment to Five things a web developer needs to know about the xAPI",http://
beta.curatr3.com/courses/xapi/home#object/11934,"Five things a web developer needs to know
about the xAPI",http://adlnet.gov/expapi/verbs/commented
ecb21e93-a30d-4f97-bdc9-7f03f4c3e136,http://beta.curatr3.com/courses/xapi/home#object/
11934,"Five things a web developer needs to know about the xAPI",null,null,http://adlnet.gov/
expapi/verbs/completed
0214340b-22cd-4c95-88a7-3de483a965cf,http://beta.curatr3.com/courses/xapi/learn,"Learn xAPI -
Learn",null,null,http://activitystrea.ms/schema/1.0/access
7ddd70ac-5b1d-4f6c-a190-8ec463875b13,http://beta.curatr3.com/courses/xapi/learn,"Learn xAPI -
Learn",null,null,http://activitystrea.ms/schema/1.0/access
f25cb81d-caff-43a6-a234-ba74b5256dc4,http://beta.curatr3.com/courses/xapi/learn,"Learn xAPI -
Learn",null,null,http://activitystrea.ms/schema/1.0/access
c4fda54d-46f2-4737-8ae9-d855d92a3bd2,http://beta.curatr3.com/courses/xapi/learn,"Learn xAPI -
Learn",null,null,http://activitystrea.ms/schema/1.0/access
6692b056-9ead-47ab-a7e2-0ac6a60bbbed,http://beta.curatr3.com/courses/xapi/home#object/
11973,"Week One Problem Solution",null,null,http://adlnet.gov/expapi/verbs/completed
e8632e21-f95c-4428-9c7a-83269725f0ab,http://beta.curatr3.com/courses/xapi/learn,"Learn xAPI -
Learn",null,null,http://activitystrea.ms/schema/1.0/access
2059fc5c-89ca-4bbf-a997-5512c045d1b4,http://beta.curatr3.com/courses/xapi/learn,"Learn xAPI -
Learn",null,null,http://activitystrea.ms/schema/1.0/access
18737298-ab08-4a9e-8267-6ca5f20ea1e2,http://beta.curatr3.com/courses/xapi/learn,"Learn xAPI -
Learn",null,null,http://activitystrea.ms/schema/1.0/access
```

Opening the file in a spreadsheet will at least put the data into a familiar format, but that's just the starting point:

	A	B	C	D	E	F	G	H
1	id	object-id	object-name	parent-id	parent-name	verb-id		
2	3dd108ac-7a41-4d7b-a01f-b45	http://beta.c	Building a Learning Record Store	null	null	http://adlnet.gov/expapi/verbs/completed		
3	b531a370-ab1e-49c9-9b7d-5c	http://beta.c	comment to Five things a web developer needs t	http://beta.c	Five things a	http://adlnet.gov/expapi/verbs/commente		
4	ecb21e93-a30d-4f97-bdc9-7f0	http://beta.c	Five things a web developer needs to know abou	null	null	http://adlnet.gov/expapi/verbs/completed		
5	0214340b-22cd-4c95-88a7-3d	http://beta.c	Learn xAPI - Learn	null	null	http://activitystrea.ms/schema/1.0/access		
6	7ddd70ac-5b1d-4f6c-a190-8ec	http://beta.c	Learn xAPI - Learn	null	null	http://activitystrea.ms/schema/1.0/access		
7	f25cb81d-caff-43a6-a234-ba74	http://beta.c	Learn xAPI - Learn	null	null	http://activitystrea.ms/schema/1.0/access		
8	c4fda54d-46f2-4737-8ae9-d85	http://beta.c	Learn xAPI - Learn	null	null	http://activitystrea.ms/schema/1.0/access		
9	6692b056-9ead-47ab-a7e2-0a	http://beta.c	Week One Problem Solution	null	null	http://adlnet.gov/expapi/verbs/completed		
10	e8632e21-f95c-4428-9c7a-832	http://beta.c	Learn xAPI - Learn	null	null	http://activitystrea.ms/schema/1.0/access		
11	2059fc5c-89ca-4bbf-a997-551	http://beta.c	Learn xAPI - Learn	null	null	http://activitystrea.ms/schema/1.0/access		
12	18737298-ab08-4a9e-8267-6c	http://beta.c	Learn xAPI - Learn	null	null	http://activitystrea.ms/schema/1.0/access		
13	c75d7dbb-eb1e-4351-818c-0f	http://beta.c	Learn xAPI - Learn	null	null	http://activitystrea.ms/schema/1.0/access		
14	34365b87-55e1-4848-88e3-bf	http://beta.c	Learn xAPI - Learn	null	null	http://activitystrea.ms/schema/1.0/access		
15	20127a81-2e20-4b6c-ac9b-fba	http://beta.c	LEARN xAPI Twitter list	null	null	http://adlnet.gov/expapi/verbs/completed		
16	c419f782-3714-47c0-b9a8-0d3	http://beta.c	Welcome to Learn xAPI	null	null	http://adlnet.gov/expapi/verbs/completed		
17	f6ec832b-7c51-43a1-9d70-ab3	http://beta.c	What are you hoping to get from this experience	null	null	http://adlnet.gov/expapi/verbs/completed		
18	ca3241d7-7b15-4122-86c0-99	http://beta.c	Introducing the Experience Hub	null	null	http://adlnet.gov/expapi/verbs/completed		
19	99cd7cac-af7c-4d2b-a31a-e36	http://beta.c	Introducing the Experience Hub	null	null	http://adlnet.gov/expapi/verbs/completed		
20	093e6332-9d24-4ede-8211-ac	http://beta.c	Welcome to the xAPI MOOC	null	null	http://adlnet.gov/expapi/verbs/completed		
21	759a4527-4682-4113-b024-28	http://beta.c	Learn xAPI - Learn	null	null	http://activitystrea.ms/schema/1.0/access		
22	087b33e9-9f2e-4d57-9c49-17(	http://beta.c	What's in a name?	null	null	http://adlnet.gov/expapi/verbs/completed		
23	82b98aff-7dda-4f13-9657-001	http://beta.c	Experience API Demystified	null	null	http://adlnet.gov/expapi/verbs/completed		
24	9f6a9327-e895-4e0c-a65d-77E	http://beta.c	Learn xAPI - Learn	null	null	http://activitystrea.ms/schema/1.0/access		
25	cb335efd-405c-419e-9e81-222	http://beta.c	xAPI in Action	null	null	http://adlnet.gov/expapi/verbs/completed		

In the world of xAPI, data can be even messier. The good thing about xAPI, however, is that we can work with data from a wide variety of sources. This is also the bad thing about xAPI. In the example above, we have data from just one source, so the columns align and the formatting is consistent. The same principles apply, regardless of the variety of data we are using. But when we have multiple data sources, the time and effort required to get things into a workable format tends to multiply.

Faced with a mass of data, we may understand why we need to give our data a good once-over before doing analysis. The question is then, "How do I do that?"

As it turns out, the process is fairly simple. Four basic steps will usually get things in good shape for analysis:

- Take a Sense Check
- Do some Data Cleaning
- Find your Center(s)
- Look at the Spread

Sense Check

Look at your data; it's like week–old milk – you'll want to check and see if it "smells right."

Inconsistencies or unexpected values can tell us that something went wrong in the data collection or the queries, and where there might be problems with data formatting or completeness.

Look at the number of data points – is it close to what you expected? Does it make sense, given the number of users, the data set you are searching, and the information you are seeking?

If we have a course with 300 users, and the data indicates 1000 views of a video, we will want to make sure that we've set up the data query the way we intended. We will also want to verify that we've set up data collection properly. In this case we might ask, what was the triggering event for the xAPI statement "N viewed X"?. Was it that the users navigated to the page where the video is located, they hit play and watched the video for a minimum amount of time, or watched it from beginning to end? If we don't know what specific event created the statement, it will be impossible to interpret the data in a meaningful or valid way.

We would also take a look at the content and determine whether this video would typically generate repeat views. In other words, if all those viewed statements were verified events, we want to know if there's a logical (or common) reason why this occurred. Was the material complex? Was the video quality poor? Was it material that functions as a performance guide or reference for other parts of the course?

In some cases, multiple views mean that something is working poorly; in others it means the object is working exactly as it was intended. We'll know what's happening when we explore some underlying context and details.

Similarly, it's important to look at the range of data, as well as the maximum and minimum values. If they don't make sense given what we know about the activities and users that are behind that data, then we'll want to take time to find out why, before preceding. The time and effort we spend will be more than repaid. These basic sense checks help confirm that we got the data we intended to request, and we'll know this before we start getting into analysis.

Chapter 8 covered the importance of understanding the activities and transactions that underlie your data. Doing a sense-check of your data is going to give you your first experience of why that is important, and will often be your first opportunity to get a real sense of the effectiveness and flaws in your data collection plan. Often, simple inconsistencies in metadata, context, or statement design can lead to misleading results from seemingly good queries.

This preliminary exploration helps us to discover the weaknesses in our existing processes and procedures and to make improvements that will maximize quality and usefulness. We will discuss how to manage our data in detail in the section on Data Stewardship in Chapter 12, but for the moment we'll continue to look at some basics.

A final step we can take in our preliminary look at a data set is to plot the data. Even a simple scatterplot or line chart is sufficient to convey a visual sense of what is going on and to gain a sense of what we might want to examine.

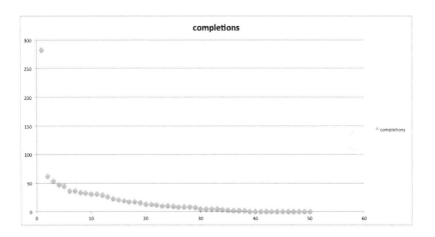

Cleaning

Even if the data seems to make sense in terms of range and the number of points, it's likely that it won't be perfectly usable when we first get it. After all, data is messy (for a lot of reasons), and so if we've done our sense check and feel confident that our queries did what they intended, and we have the data we need, we will need to clean it.

There's nothing particularly mystical or mysterious about data cleaning. It can be time-consuming, but it's another step we need to take to make sure any analysis we do gives us meaningful results.

We're basically extending our general sense check into some specifics, for even with machine generated data there will be inconsistencies when we are looking at data from a variety of sources. Typical problem areas are:

- Date formats
- Names
- Units
- Duplicate data
- Missing data

Much of this can (and needs to) be managed within the data collection process. Designing statements well and planning carefully around user names and other details can go a long way toward having good-quality data from the start. But the reality is usually not ideal. We might have well-designed statements but a system set-up that allows users to use non-unique IDs or create (often inadvertently) multiple log-ins to the same course. We might find that when a user re-visits a completed object, the course sends another completion statement for the same object (an effect we might or might not want, depending on our needs).

We've discussed xAPI profiles, as well as the need to really understand the activities that create your data; keeping those details in mind can help you with some of your data cleaning. Beyond that, it's a matter your time and attention. If things don't look right, it's worth seeing if it's a problem with the data or if it's something that is, in fact, right, but that you didn't know about or anticipate. To help determine whether the data makes sense, after you've looked at the typical problem areas mentioned above, you'll want to do a little more systematic exploration of your data.

And of course, if we're adopting xAPI in part because of an interest in interoperability and because we want to look at learning- and performance-related data from outside the LMS, we start to see where data cleaning becomes critical. It can be something as basic as managing different User IDs on different platforms, or recognizing that we want to add some relevant metadata to our xAPI statements to facilitate analysis of data from outside the LMS. Or perhaps we realize that we have some data sources that use UTC exclusively, while others have timestamps based on the time zone where the data was created. More data sources can mean more effort and more complexity, and much of how the data is structured may be outside of our control. But being aware of our data needs and the potential issues in our data supply chain will help streamline data cleaning and will drive improvements to reduce data quality issues in the future.

Once we've done the sense check, and the data cleaning, it's time to start digging in and getting to know our data.

Centers and Spread

One of the main things we want to know about our data is, where is the center? Consider some common questions that are asked:

What was the average time spent on site?
What was the average score on this assessment?
What is the typical number of objects views, or tasks completed, per user?

These are reasonable questions to ask, but we need to approach our answers with care. When people talk about the "average" of a data set, they generally mean the center, but the question is, which center?

The Mean

Our mental default for the center of data is the mean, expressed by the equation:

$$\bar{x} = \frac{\sum x_i}{n}$$

Even if you don't recognize the equation, you know the approach as you've probably been doing this since elementary school: add up all values and then divide that sum by the number of values.

But that's only one way to measure the data. If you let

your brain drift back to middle school math, you might recall that there are two other measures of center:

The Median

This is the central value of all your numbers if you list them in order. For example, if you have a set of numbers:

1, 2, 2, 2, 4, 5, 5, 6, 8

The median is 4

The Mode

This the most frequently occurring value in a set of numbers. In the case of the set above, it would be 2.

Each of these measures of center has

Normal Distribution

The mean works well if our data is distributed like this:

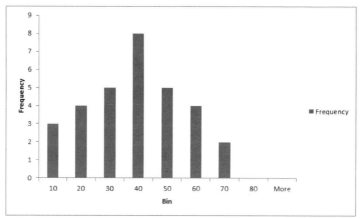

A normal distribution is that ideal bell-curve where data is evenly distributed around the center. A normal distribution makes life easy: the Mean, Median, and Mode are all the same number. Or, in the real world where a perfect distribution is unlikely, a normal distribution at least has central values that are so close to one another that it really doesn't matter which one we use. Quite often, though, we may find that our data does not have a normal distribution.

Skewed Data

What if our data looks like this?

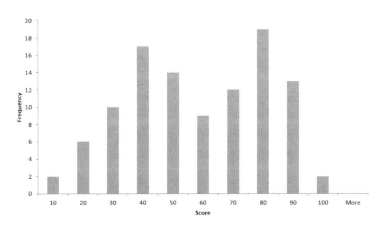

The mean won't tell you a lot here. If this were data about participation or performance in a course (instead of insect body length), the center of the data would not be as interesting as the fact that users either did very well or very poorly. A situation like this is an invitation to explore more deeply to find out why. But if we had looked only at the center of the data, not the distribution, we might have missed out on some important insights.

The mean also won't tell you much if your data is skewed. Skewed data is data in which the distribution of outcomes is heavily shifted to the higher or lower values with a long, but shallow, tail of outliers. Skewed data is not uncommon in the real world, both in learning data and in general. It is one of the more typical patterns we might see when looking at data about typical points of interest like completions or time spent on a portal.

A scatterplot might look something like this:

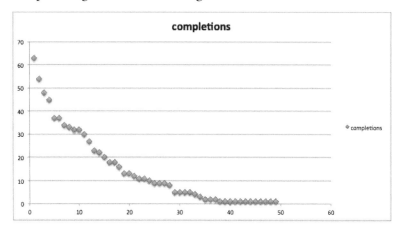

With a frequency plot (histogram looking like this)

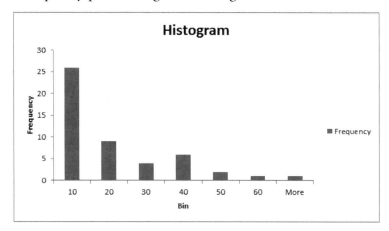

In this case, the mean isn't going to tell us very much about the center of the data. But it tells us some interesting things about the data. Both multi-modal (more than one center) and skewed data sets are pointers to some potentially interesting realities that underlie our data. Let's say we're looking at some assessment results and we have a bimodal data set:

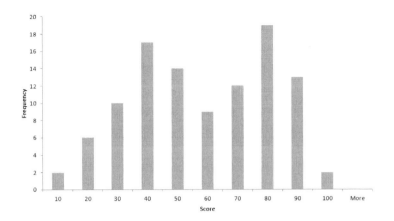

This tells us that people either really grasped what was being assessed or were struggling; there wasn't a lot of middle ground. It's a more realistic view of the data than simply taking the mean; it gives much more useful information. Thus, knowing that there is disparity in the results prompts us to explore why the disparity happened and to build plans for improvement.

It is worth discussing how to deal with centers where data is skewed as it was in the completions data above, but first we should look at one more key concept: spread.

Spread

Understanding the spread of our data set (that is, how widely the values vary) is important for two reasons. First, spread tells us something about our data set. If, for example, we are looking at data about assessment scores on a 100 point scale, and the range of scores is 20 points from max to min, this means something different from a 80 point spread. A larger spread can lead to some interesting questions about why there's a significant variance, which can lead to insights that are related, perhaps, to our users' needs, or the course design. It's another opportunity to look at how users have performed and how the course has performed.

Turning to a real world data set, we can get a feel for what centers and spread look like in the real world and how to find outliers. Outliers are those data points that are so numerically distant from the main data set that they are probably not realistic or meaningful and should not be included in the assessment. For example, in a data set where we looked at the average time spent on portal, one of the users had over 17 continuous hours while the majority of users had sessions of 15-45 minutes. This makes it clear that the 17 hour figure was not realistic; it was an outlier. Knowing how xAPI statements were generated for time spent on the portal as well as some details of the course design, we were able to determine the source of that outlier, and to recognize that it was not a relevant point in determining typical time spent or the real spread of the data.

Example Analysis

To see how centers, spread, and outliers play out in the real world, let's consider some (non-learning) data: Major League Soccer salaries from 2015 (a publically available data set), which documents 570 salaries ranging from $50,000 to over $7 Million.

This histogram shows the distribution of salaries along with our three measures of center:

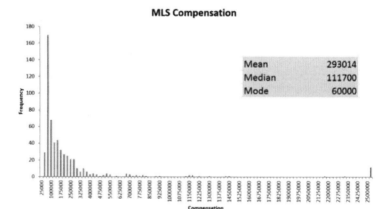

From a quick glance it is clear that this data set is skewed; indeed, our three measures of center confirm it.

The Mean is approximately 2.5 times greater than the Median, and almost 5 times greater than the Mode.

When we look at the range of numbers ($50,000 - $7,000,00) along with the distribution of the data, it's very easy to see how much the Mean can be influenced by outliers. Now, in this case it's not that the outliers (the very high salaries) are poor data, but they are not meaningful or representative if you are trying to figure out the typical standard of living for an MLS player (for example, if you happen to be a mortgage lender or a loan officer at a bank).

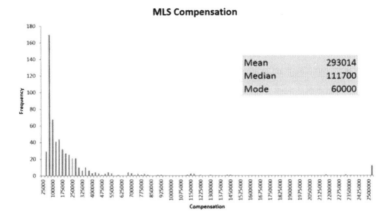

Meanwhile, the median (the central value of all the 570 data points) seems, visually, more realistic – and in fact, the median is usually the recommended value for centers in skewed data sets.

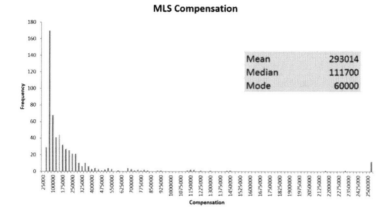

The Mode of $60,000 is not terribly surprising – there are a lot of players just squeaking by – and it might be useful to know that it's a common salary. Similarly, in learning, we might want to know the central score, but we might also want to know what the most common score is, even if it's not central.

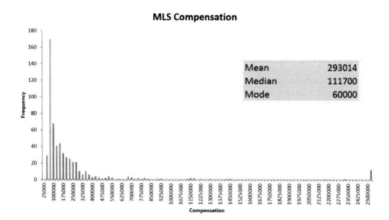

Handling Outliers

But what if we want to get rid of those outliers?
How do we decide what's relevant?
There are a couple of common approaches:

If you calculate the mean, you will also typically calculate the standard deviation: σ (this can be done fairly quickly using the descriptive statistics tools in most spreadsheets. Typically if a number is more than three standard deviations (3σ) away from the mean, it is considered an outlier. This approach is quick, but there is the obvious weakness that it relies on the Mean, which, as discussed above, is influenced by outliers (which is a bit of a catch-22 with respect to outlier detection). However, if you need just a quick overview of your data and not high levels of statistical accuracy, it's a fairly useful approach.

A more involved and more accurate approach involves using the Median and the Interquartile Range. It's not difficult but it does involve a few more steps. This is sometimes known as the Five Number Summary. If you'd like to learn more about it, there's an excellent summary at https://faculty.elgin.edu/dkernler/statistics/ch03/3-5.html.

When we remove the outliers from our data set, we see that the Mean changes to a much more plausible $163,000.

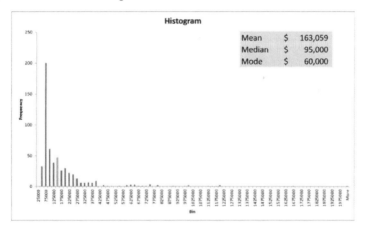

While we don't need a deep background in statistics to start finding some interesting insights in our data sets, we do need to be aware, at least, of outliers, because of their impact on measuring the center of our data and because we want to know why they are there. Sometimes it's bad data (as we found in the time spent on site data).

This is called a logical or functional outlier; the data itself is not valid, either because of problems with collection, or some other factor that renders a data point meaningless. Those sorts of outliers are another reason why understanding, cleaning, and exploring our data are so important; it's essential to know when and how logical outliers happen, so that we can account for them in our analysis, and so that we can try to improve our processes to avoid them in the future.

Sometimes outliers are due to exceptional cases (as seen in the salary data), these are called statistical outliers. The data may be valid, but the individual data points are not representative of the general case. Statistical outliers are important for several reasons: first, because it's interesting to understand why and how some people get results that are much better or much worse than the rest of the population. Knowing the factors that help create those sorts of differences can inform future design, either by pointing out previously unconsidered opportunities, or by helping to build improvements that avoid potential pitfalls. Outliers are one more way not only to improve analysis, but to improve our understanding of our data and to begin to discover new avenues of data exploration.

Getting Started with Analysis

Once we've done the basic cleaning and exploration of data, to make sure that what we have is reasonable, and once we understand what the numbers mean in terms of real world events, we can start looking for new insights from our data.

At this point understanding the questions we're asking is as important as understanding our data. In the case of sales training, we were asked to provide some information on the participation; in particular, the question was "What are the most popular objects in this course?" Given that this was on a social learning platform, the question wasn't as straightforward as it appeared. Did "most popular" mean:

- Most viewed?
- Most commented on?
- Most discussed (comments and replies)?

- Most recommended?
- All of the above?

After cleaning and exploring our data, we were able to consider the different ways to measure popularity, look at points of convergence and divergence, and decide which factors were relevant. But often it is the data exploration itself that points us to new questions we might not have even thought to consider. We wanted to explore whether a change in the user interface increased participation in conversations within a social learning platform. After we prepared the data and started analyzing it, we soon noticed that if we defined increased discussion as "more comments," then the UI changes had no significant effect, positive or negative. But when we looked at not just comments but at replies to those comments, we saw a clear 12% increase. For social learning, improving the rates of actual conversations (replies) was a gratifying finding, but it also reminded us that even with good quality data, we need to understand which activities trigger which statements, and we need to be well grounded in the data's context if we are going get anything of value from it.

After we did the initial analysis, we started thinking about some trends that seemed to be emerging during the initial data exploration, and we decided to pull a bit more data so that we could look at conversation in relation to completion of levels within the course (the course had time-locked levels, rather than completion-locked, so participation in Level 3, for example, was not contingent upon completion of Level 2). This particular course had two parallel tracks: one was highly technical, the other was focused on business strategy, and the difference in trends of conversation relative to completion was quite interesting.

In the more technical track, those who were involved in the social aspect of the course (discussion of learning objects) were likely to complete levels that those who weren't conversing weren't completing. Obviously there's no causality proven: it may be that those committed enough to complete the complex material were going to be fully engaged, or perhaps the support and engagement of fellow learners were key elements to mastery of complex material. It was an interesting finding that merited deeper examination, but what merits our attention now is that it was a question that arose only during that initial exploration of data.

Interestingly, the non-technical track of the course had very different trends as far as participation in conversation and completions: there were a number of users commenting and clearly engaged who did not complete specific levels of the course. They were engaged and enthusiastic, but from a business strategy perspective, qualitative data suggested that there was more interest in exploring some key concepts for future application and considering them within practical application, and less assumption of a need to master all concepts. The context and content of the strategy track was such that curating a small subset of concepts was sufficient for users to move forward in their understanding and application, in contrast with the technical track where skipping over details would leave potential critical gaps for implementation.

The findings were interesting, and not what we were looking for initially. Data exploration sets us up for a kind of planned serendipity. The effort to clean and to understand our data makes us more closely familiar with it. This makes us more likely to spot useful trails to follow, giving us new insights into how our courses are working and how users engage with them.

For this long chapter, these are the short take-aways:

Things go wrong with data, in many ways, and so you need to know what brought the data into being:

- How were statements designed?
- What activities create statements? (e.g. What does "completed" mean in the real world?)
- What are the sources and formats of data from different platforms?
- What metadata do we have? (And what metadata do we need?)

Data exploration is vital if we want to find potential issues in our data. Do the number of data points look reasonable? Does the range of the data make sense? Are there duplicates or missing data? (Etc.) It is also how we start seeing trends and finding new questions to ask. In other words, it's the first step to insight into what's really going on.

References

Ambler, Scott. "Data Modeling 101." Agile Data. Accessed January 26, 2017. www.agiledata.org/essays/dataModeling101.html.

Angrist, Joshua David, and Jörn-Steffen Pischke. *Mostly Harmless Econometrics: An Empiricist's Companion.* Princeton: Princeton University Press, 2009.

Baum, David. "Data Quality, Data Governance, and Master Data Management (MDM)." Oracle | Integrated Cloud Applications and Platform Services. Accessed January 26, 2017. http://www.oracle.com/us/c-central/cio-solutions/information-matters/importance-of-data/index.html.

Few, Stephen. *Information Dashboard Design Displaying Data for at-a-Glance Monitoring.* Burlingame, California: Analytics press, 2013.

Fleisher, Craig S., and Babette E. Bensoussan. *Business and Competitive Analysis: Effective Application of New and Classic Methods.* Upper Saddle River, NJ: Financial Times Press, 2007.

Harnett, Donald L., and Ashok Soni. *Statistical methods for business and economics.* Reading, Mass. [etc.]: Addison-Wesley, 1991.

Heuer, Jr., Richards J. "Psychology of Intelligence Analysis." Central Intelligence Agency. Last modified 1999. https://www.cia.gov/library/center-for-the-study-of-intelligence/csi-publications/books-and-monographs/psychology-of-intelligence-analysis/PsychofIntelNew.pdf.

Hoberman, Steve. *Data Modeling Made Simple: A Practical Guide for Business and IT Professionals.* Bradley Beach, N.J.: Technics Publications, 2009.

Howson, Cindi. *Successful Business Intelligence: Unlock the Value of BI & Big Data, Second Edition.* McGraw-Hill/Osborne, 2013.

Schutt, Cathy O'Neil. Rachel. *Doing Data Science.* Sebastopol, CA: O'Reilly Media, Inc, 2013.

Siegel, Eric. *Predictive Analytics The Power to Predict Who Will Click, Buy, Lie, or Die.* Hoboken, New Jersey: John Wiley & Sons, Inc, 2013.

Zumel, Nina, and John Mount. *Practical Data Science with R.* Shelter Island, NY: Manning Publications, 2014.

Chapter 9

Beyond the Basics

Sometimes the basic data exploration we discussed in Chapter 8 will provide the insights we're looking for, but sometimes we'll need to do some more involved analysis – not necessarily rocket science, but work that takes us a bit beyond basic spreadsheets. Data analysis and statistics are fields that can take years to master; fortunately, with a few straightforward approaches we can address some issues of interest to learning professionals.

Even basic approaches require some extra time and care, of course, because with data analysis it remains very easy to get things wrong. So why bother with all this? Let's hear what learning professionals have to say:

> *"We know they've been trained to do it, but can they actually do it?"*

> *"When L&D professionals can provide data and analysis linked to strategy, they will be a key influencer."*

> *"I don't think HR or L&D need to worry about the seat or playing second fiddle. Simply provide the data analysis that drives solid decision making for the organization and deliver the needed services."*

In other words, we need to keep our overarching business goals in mind when we work with learning data; we're looking for insights that will guide action.

Probably when you were back in elementary school you were assigned the exercise of writing a lead paragraph for a news article. You had to come up with the 5 W's – Who, What, When, Where, and Why. As it happens, xAPI data gives us that basic information, and we can use it to tell a story. Some of the more common questions we're asked revolve around the "When". Details of time can be trivial if they amount to nothing more than a bean-counting exercise, but in other instances they can be a source of great insight about user needs and course effectiveness. Time to Competence, or understanding how users interact with a course or a learning object – these are examples of ways that we can take data around time and turn it into actionable insights.

Navigation and Interaction Patterns

One of the most basic approaches is to use timelines to understand how our users interact with our courses. For a recent non-linear course, we were curious to see how users navigated through the learning objects. Would they take advantage of the opportunity for free-range learning, or would they go with the familiar approach of working through the learning objects in sequential order?

By mapping order of object views against course object numbers, we came up with some interesting insights.

A majority of users navigated through the course primarily in sequential order, with occasional checks back to previously viewed content. This was, in a way, unsurprising – going through a list of objects in order is commonly the default approach to reading or learning. What was more interesting was our finding that those who proceeded through the course linearly could be divided into two subgroups: those who went through the course almost entirely in object order, with only a few return visits to previously viewed objects, and those for whom 20% of their object views were revisits to previously viewed objects. There was a third, less common approach to the course: those who took full adventure of the non-linear nature and followed no immediately obvious sequence in their order of object views.

Perhaps these results are not terribly surprising; it's a fairly normal situation to have a few general approaches to learning, some more obviously structured than others. But having the data made the patterns evident and opened up opportunities to dive more deeply into the "why?" and the "what next?"

- Did the order of viewing objects affect performance? Did revision of certain objects affect performance?
- Were some objects re-viewed more than others, and if so why?
- If users reviewed certain objects, was it actually for learning purposes or, since this was a web-based

course, was it just navigating to the URL that would autofill when they started typing the course address?

- Was there a difference in prior subject matter expertise between those who navigated linearly, and those who navigated non-linearly?

In the end, the basic question, "Do people navigate a course in sequential order, even if they are not required to?" led us to look more deeply into how our users interact with the course. We could explore what elements of the course were revisited by accident, or because new information of interest triggered a second look. We gained an idea about which course elements might prove challenging, and which objects are most useful for which users. By using quantitative and qualitative data together to explore the reason behind the numbers, we were ultimately able to create a feedback loop so that we could modify course design to improve performance results.

What is time spent, really?

Often when it comes to time or timelines, what we get asked is something basic and pragmatic:

How much time did the users spend on (an object) (a session) (the course)(achieving a competency)?

What does that mean? What might we or our stakeholders really be asking?

"Time Spent on a Session" is one of the data requests we see most often. To answer it well, we need to go back to the kinds of basic questions we've discussed in earlier chapters:

- Why do we want to know this?
  - o What's the question we are trying to answer?
  - o What decisions or actions do we hope to take in response to the data?

It might be that we need to know how much time a course

typically requires to complete successfully, or it might
be that we are being asked to document the trends in
learner engagement over the duration of a course.

Using time spent to demonstrate engagement is a bit tricky. First
of all, it's a rather tenuous leap to correlate time with engagement,
especially if we are considering it as a sole factor, in isolation from
other corroborating data. But even in a situation where we have
been requested to look at time spent on learning as one data set
among several others, in a well-planned analysis of user engagement,
we're not home free. We may have defined our data goal, and
the data needed to meet that goal, but we need to makes sure we
have also defined how we're actually measuring "time spent."

Going back to our basic questions around data we need to know:

How is the data documenting "time spent" created?
- What user or system actions generate
  the numbers we plan to use?
    o Do we need to do anything to
      make that data usable?

We need to know how our xAPI statements are set up to measure
time; what specific actions create the start and end point of an
activity or session; and how likely we are to have junk data.

In the case of time-related data, one of the biggest sources of junk
is a situation where a session is considered active purely on the
basis of log-in and log-out times. We need to know if a session
times out after inactivity, and if so, what that time-out point is.
Ideally we have this information, or we can ask someone for it. In
the real world, though, we may get data from a variety of sources,
some of which give us no control and no ability to see the processes
behind the data. In such a situation we have to fall back on what
we can discover in initial data exploration. Maybe we have a few
outliers that are totally outrageous (as we saw in Chapter 8). Or
maybe we have a surprising number of people with session times
of precisely 10 minutes, which might hint to us the existence of
a 10-minute session time-out window. This is something we can

verify, if necessary, by reviewing the data carefully; did those users with the identical, precise session times have any other statements other than logging in and logging out in that time window?

Timelines are a useful and generally simple way to start getting value from our learning data, but it's vital to remain thoughtful about the data we are using and the underlying goals of our analysis.

If This, Then That? – Correlation

When we want to understand how an action or event correlates with an outcome, we can use the mathematical tool called regression analysis. Regression analysis is a way to determine the strength of the relationships between variables, allowing us to make inferences or predictions based on those relationships. There are two types of variables: dependent and independent. In a regression analysis we're trying to establish if there is a correlation between one or more independent variables and a single dependent variable.

For example, I might run a regression analysis to see if the amount of rainfall (independent variable) has any relationship to the expected yield of corn (dependent variable) for local farmers. Now there might be other independent variables I could factor in, like average daily temperatures, or the amount of fertilizer used. The main thing to understand is that we can look at one or more factors (independent variables) and see if and how they correlate with a single dependent variable.

Correlation is never 100%, and when we do regression, we're looking for "this tends to relate to that." Rainy summers tend to correlate with higher corn yields than dry summers do, at least up to a point. We can also look at the relationships of the other variables individually or collectively to see what we find.

In short, there are plenty of stats books out there, if you want to dig more deeply into how regression works and learn about the many kinds of regression that can model different situations (linear vs. non linear vs logistic; single vs multiple variables).

What we're doing here is giving you a surface overview with enough to get you started and to keep you from falling into the most common traps that might derail the value of your results.

Let's look at a linear regression in its simplest form – where we have an independent variable that we anticipate will have a linear relationship with a dependent variable.

$$y = mx + b$$

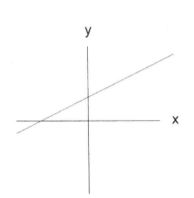

As you might remember from algebra class, x is the independent variable, y is the dependent, and m is the slope of the line, telling you how the two are correlated. If m is positive, y gets bigger as x gets bigger (as we might expect to see in the relationship between corn yield and rainfall). If m is negative, y decreases as x increases (as we might see in the relationship between new loan applications and interest rates).

Even in its simplest form regression can give us some useful insights. Maybe we'd like to see if the number of completions of course modules (independent variable) leads to an increase in sales revenue (dependent variable). Now the first rule of regression is to remember that correlation does not guarantee causation. We can, however, use correlation as a base or impetus for investigating causal relationships. Evidence to confirm or deny the causality will come from other statistical data, qualitative data, and often a healthy dose of common sense. Which is not to say that we can rely on instinct or empirical observation to prove causality, but our common sense can tell us when the results are likely quite wrong (e.g. we know that increased rainfall is not likely to benefit corn yield indefinitely, for at some point it will flood the field).

Let's look at a basic example. We're going to cheat a little and use a created data set, which is fairly idealized, just to make things a bit simpler to interpret. Suppose we designers are trying to incorporate the Community of Inquiry model into our learning design. We have a new course that includes community discussion questions, and we'd like to see if there is any correlation between users' participation in these conversations and users' retention and application of the material.

So we pull a data set that includes the user IDs, the number of contributions made, and the performance on a knowledge assessment.

	A	B	C
1	User ID	contributions	knowledge_assessment
2	1	6	79
3	2	4	76
4	3	19	83
5	4	17	81
6	5	18	87
7	6	19	86
8	7	2	78
9	8	15	90
10	9	29	98
11	10	26	97
12	11	3	75
13	12	7	76
14	13	28	99
15	14	28	96
16	15	24	97
17	16	28	97
18	17	12	81
19	18	25	97
20	19	25	94
21	20	12	83
22	21	23	89
23	22	4	76
24	23	7	76
25	24	21	86

We run a regression using a commonly available spreadsheet application and we get some outputs, some of which look slightly familiar, while others are a bit confusing.

This graph shows the actual data in blue, with the x-axis (horizontal) showing the independent variable (the number of contributions to the online discussion for a given student), while the y-axis (vertical) shows the dependent variable (assessment results for each student). The red points are the predicted values of the assessment results for each value of contribution counts.

contributions Line Fit Plot

◆ knowledge_assessment   ■ Predicted knowledge_assessment

In a regression, the model creates its prediction by minimizing the total distance of the fitted line (the red points) and the real world data. For this to be valid we need to make sure some basic standards are met.

First, do we have a sufficiently sized data sample, and is the data reliable? One of the best things about xAPI is that it makes data collection easy, so adequate sample size is not a problem. Even so, the validity of the data is going to hinge on making sure the data set is unbiased – and by unbiased, we mean having a sample of data that represents the entire population. If we are analyzing data for a course for new managers across a global organization, we want to make sure that we have a balanced data set across regions and across functional roles. With xAPI it's simple enough to collect the data, but suppose we are doing analysis from a pilot study that focuses solely on people from engineering? It would not be valid to use the results from that test to make predictions for other professional roles.

Bias can also come into play when we are evaluating data for an individual. In such a case we might do analysis with a larger spectrum of data (performance data, participation data, etc.) to give more depth to the correlations we model for that individual.

The other question we have to consider is, how far can we extend our predictions beyond a sample data set? The answer is: not very far.

A regression model is valid only for the range of data it has. In our example the maximum number of contributions to discussions points is 30. We cannot validly extend the projection to estimate what the likely test scores would be for someone who made 40 contributions.

While the linear graph above is a helpful way to visualize the general trend, we need to look at the numeric outputs from the regression to know how confident we should be about the correlation's validity.

There's a lot to see in a regression output. It's a topic to explore in depth if you choose (see the references at the end of the chapter for some good starting points), a few simple elements can get us off to a good start, and these are highlighted in green on the spreadsheet below.

Let's first take a look at R-squared, an indicator of how well our linear model fits the data. R stands for Residual, or the distance between the estimated values (the red points on the graph above) and the actual value of the data. The lower the residual, the better the fit. We can see the graph illustrating the residuals for each data point in the sample data we used to create the regression.

R-squared uses the residuals to determine the ratio of variation that is explained by the model compared to the overall variation of the data. If R-squared = 1, the model completely explains the variation in the dependent variable. If it is zero, it doesn't explain it at all. Generally speaking the closer R-squared is to 1, the better. There are a lot of caveats around this if you start getting serious about regression, but for our purposes it's a decent rule of thumb.

In our case the R-Squared value is about 0.8, so our model looks pretty good. (Since we created this data set, that's not unexpected, of course.)

	A	B	C	D	E	F	G	H	I	J
1	SUMMARY OUTPUT									
2										
3	*Regression Statistics*									
4	Multiple R	0.892228								
5	R Square	0.7960714								
6	Adjusted R Squar	0.79399								
7	Standard Error	3.398614								
8	Observations	100								
9										
10	ANOVA									
11		*df*	*SS*							
12	Regression	1	4418							
13	Residual	98	1131							
14	Total	99	5550.75							
15										
16		*Coefficients*	*Standard Error*	*t Stat*	*P-value*	*Lower 95%*	*Upper 95%*	*ower 95.0%*	*Upper 95.0%*	
17	Intercept	72.78295	0.67324291	108.108008	9.6E-104	71.44692	74.11898	71.44692	74.11898	
18	contributions	0.7866471	0.04021888	19.5591488	1.31E-35	0.706834	0.86646	0.706834	0.86646	
19										

Residual plot chart titled "contributions Residual Plot" with Residuals on the y-axis (ranging -8 to 10) and contributions on the x-axis (ranging 0 to 35).

The other numbers we want to consider are the Coefficient and the p-value. The Coefficient is simple – it's the slope, the m in our y=mx+b equation. In this case it is positive with a value of 0.79, meaning that for every additional discussion contribution a user makes, we would expect a 0.79 point increase on their assessment score.

The P-value is a way of measuring how likely it is that the model fits the data purely out of chance – this is called the null hypothesis. As part of the regression analysis, the null hypothesis is tested and the result is the P-value; the lower it is, the less likely it is that the regression result is due to dumb luck. In our case the P-value is effectively zero ($1.3 * 10^{-23}$) so we can reject the null hypothesis.

To sum up, the R-squared tells us how well the model fits, the

P-value tells us how likely it is to be statistically meaningful. In any regression we perform, we need to look at both.

When a number is not a number

When we're looking at a spreadsheet it's easy to forget that sometimes a number in our data set does not represent a numeric value; sometimes numbers are categorical data. They might be ordinal numbers, or numbers to classify ("small, medium, large" denoted as "1, 2, 3"). If we try to do a linear regression on categories, things will fall apart quickly. It is still possible to model this kind of data, using tools like cluster analysis or logistic regression. Such methods take time, effort, and math to understand and use effectively, but they can yield some very useful results. (We'll discuss an example later in this chapter.) It's a matter of weighing the cost and benefit for your particular needs and goals.

If nothing else, it's a good reminder that we need to approach statistical methods with care. We want to be precise about data; similarly we want to be precise about the use cases for various statistical analyses. The fact that many statistical tools can be accessed with the click of a few keys on a spreadsheet means that we can quickly get ourselves into trouble if we don't take care to understand a tool, its requirements, its valid applications, and how to interpret its results.

And yet although we need to proceed with informed caution when doing data analysis, we've arrived at the point where we can begin to get some interesting and useful results, results that can generate meaningful feedback for our design processes and for our learners, perhaps even results that we can use to demonstrate not only correlation, but cause.

Tying Quantitative and Qualitative Together

Learning data presents some significant challenges when it comes to analysis. It's not like a chemistry experiment where we can test hypotheses in controlled settings. Our users have numerous and ever changing variables with respect to learning, depending maybe on a conversation over coffee, a journal article read, a workshop attended, or a change in leadership. Our users have experiences that affect their knowledge and their motivation, and most of these are well outside the sphere of what we can control or even easily measure.

We're not the only field facing this situation. Medical research, especially in the realm of patient outcomes, faces similar challenges. If we are trying to understand the efficacy of a certain treatment or protocol, we can only control so many variables, and an awful lot of the data is qualitative. To compensate for this situation, we need to triangulate our data.

The term Data Triangulation is rooted in the method of determining a location by using multiple data points:

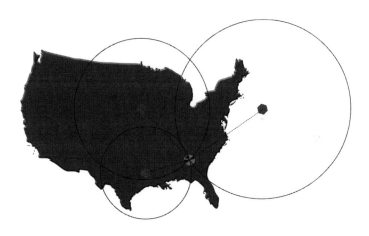

Image Credit: Urbazon Media/Shutterstock

When we talk about triangulation in research we're trying to use data from multiple sources and research methods in order to obtain a more complete and more valid analysis of correlations and, optimally, causality.

When we're trying to prove a relationship between causes and effects we evaluate evidence. Numeric data and statistical analysis provide one kind of evidence. Qualitative data, whether it be from usability studies or analysis of the content and context that underlie numeric data, is critical not just if we want more meaningful analysis but also if we wish to create a more complete set of evidence, which in turn allows us to draw more accurate conclusions, which in turn help drive more effective future actions or decisions.

We already briefly discussed this concept in our exploration of user timelines earlier in the chapter. Let's take a look at some more real world examples.

User Interface Analysis

Numeric data is great, but by itself it is not sufficient to improve the design of the User Interface (UI). We can generate numeric data about who clicked what elements, and how many times they did so, but that's not going to tell us the whole story. Moreover, it's definitely not going to give us sufficient information to inform modifications and improvements to the design. As we stated in earlier chapters, qualitative data gives the whys and hows – the critical context to flesh out the bones of our quantitative data.

We have choices about when and how to collect qualitative data. In the case of UI testing it may be optimal to collect both quantitative and qualitative data at the same time, allowing the two data sets to be directly linked. The number of clicks to perform an operation could be collected along with data from the user about what they felt worked well and what they felt did not. Then we would understand not just the clicks being made in the UI, but why the user made them. From this combined data, we can come to better decisions about design changes to the UI. Will there be times when we want to collect the data sets asynchronously? Certainly. One example of such a situation might be the initial rollout of a new course. Suppose that we open the new course, we collect quantitative data, and we discover that a significant proportion of learners are navigating through the course differently from what we expected. Based on what we know about the actual course usage, we might want to interview a set of users to see why certain paths were taken. We can then look at the data collected from the quantitative and qualitative studies to determine whether the course merits changes.

In learning intervention design we are trying to design engaging content along with user interface that is understandable and not intrusive on the content. Collecting simple quantitative data will not be enough to make sure that the interface works.

Numbers show us that learners have visited pages, clicked buttons, taken quizzes, and interacted with the content, and we've seen that we can triangulate quantitative and qualitative data to determine whether our course design is working as it should be, and how, and why.

But obviously UI design is only one piece of the puzzle – an important piece, but only one among many. We have lots of other questions to answer:

- What if only 50% of the learners interact with a piece of content? Why did they not? And does it matter, performance-wise, that they did not?
- What if only 10% are able to answer a question correctly after taking the course? Why did that happen?
- What if performance doesn't improve after taking the course?

How might we use data to determine the relationship between learning objects, user interaction with those objects, and performance?

Did It Matter

We all know that when it comes to learning, the question isn't just "Did the users do it?" It's "Did it matter that they did?" We can cite more than one data customer who has asked to explore this question in the context of social learning. In each case, their interest started with the simple question: "How much conversation is really going on for each learning object?" This quickly evolved to "Which learning objects in each module generate the most discussion?" with the implied subtext, "Are they the ones we think are most important?" This is usually followed by, "And if not, why not?"

So let's suppose we are tasked to determine if the "right" content is generating reflection and conversation (with the inferred benefit of better learning). The reality is that this question is the surface concern; it will quickly be followed by many others: If the "right" content is not doing what it was supposed to, is the problem with mastery of the content (due to its inherent substance/complexity, or possibly due to the quality of the specific resource used for that object)? Or is the problem that the content the designers decided was vital differs from what their users see as vital? If we notice little discussion of a key learning object, is the problem a matter of how the discussion questions were posed?

Finding root causes is asking a lot from an analysis, but there are ways to start narrowing things down, at least.

We can begin by collecting the obvious quantitative data:

- How many views did each object have?
- How many comments were made?
- How many replies were made to comments?

And we can explore our data, to look for outliers and trends.

Then we'd need to dig into some qualitative analysis. This is something that can be done manually. It may be time-consuming to read over even a portion of the comments, but doing so allows us to see what really resonates with users. It can be a very enlightening window into the issues and needs they face in their work. It's also possible to see that some learning objects that generate large volumes of conversation may not be generating high-quality conversation. The reason for this might be the nature of the object, or the question asked. "What's an example of this [topic] that you've encountered, and how did you manage it?" is a question that will encourage higher value comments than "Have you seen this before?"

Data triangulation will come into play when we try to figure out whether an object has failed to generate much conversation because the object is poor-quality or irrelevant. Or perhaps the associated talking point is flawed and unlikely to require or encourage real thought and reflection. Or perhaps the material is challenging, and users need more support in order to master it and make the performance improvements they are hoping to make.

When we use quantitative and qualitative data together, we find they provide vital feedback loops that can have positive impacts on course design. Those impacts might be UI improvements that help refine the learning objects for a course, based on what's relevant, what gets people excited, or what's a waste of time. And ultimately we can demonstrate whether a course is making a difference, and how we can improve course performance and learner performance, and then do so based on evidence.

References

Ambler, Scott. "Data Modeling 101." Agile Data. Accessed January 26, 2017. www.agiledata.org/essays/dataModeling101.html.

Dylan, William. *Embedded Formative Assessment.* Bloomington, IN: Solution Tree Press, 2011.

Foreman, John W. *Data Smart: Using Data Science to Transform Information into Insight.* Indianapolis: John Wiley & Sons, 2014.

Harnett, Donald L., and Ashok Soni. *Statistical methods for business and economics.* Reading, Mass. [etc.]: Addison-Wesley, 1991.

Leeb, Scott. "How Knowledge Management Drives C-Suite Decision Making." IntelCollab. Last modified November 26, 2013. http://intelcollab.com/how-knowledge-management-at-the-rockefeller-foundation-drives-c-suite-decision-making/.

Liebowitz, Jay. *Strategic Intelligence: Business Intelligence, Competitive Intelligence, and Knowledge Management.* Boca Raton: Auerbach Publications, 2006.

Macfadyen, Leah P., and Shane Dawson. "Numbers Are Not Enough. Why e-Learning Analytics Failed to Inform an Institutional Strategic Plan." Journal of Educational Technology & Society. Last modified 2012. http://ifets.info/journals/15_3/11.pdf.

Schutt, Cathy O'Neil. Rachel. *Doing Data Science.* Sebastopol, CA: O'Reilly Media, Inc, 2013.

Trochim, William M.K. "The Qualitative Debate." Social Research Methods. Last modified October 20, 2006. http://www.socialresearchmethods.net/kb/qualdeb.php.

University of California, Berkely. "Data Analysis Toolkits." UC Berkeley Seismology Lab. Accessed January 29, 2017. http://seismo.berkeley.edu/~kirchner/eps_120/EPSToolkits.htm.

"Why Are We Doing This? Asking the Right Questions of Your Learning Data." HT2 Labs. Last modified May 18, 2016. https://www.ht2labs.com/blog/asking-right-questions-learning-data/.

Chapter 10

Data Stewardship and Other Keys to Success

Data analysis is a pretty deep well to drink from. You can keep coming back for more, you can keep diving deeper. It all depends on your needs and the time you can commit to it. But there is one common element to every data project: if you don't take time to manage your data, it's going to get real messy, real fast.

There are several reasons why we need a to understand, document, and manage the systems around our data collection and data use:

- We need to know what lies beneath our data.
- We will need to be able to explain how we used our data, and why we made the decision(s) we did.
- Someone needs to have responsibility, whether implicit or explicit.

We Need to Know What Lies beneath Our Data

We've talked about this in general terms before, but knowing the activities and definitions that underlie our data is what makes it useful for deriving valid, meaningful information. It's good to create some sort of data dictionary – a summary of the events you want to record and what you need to know about them.

This can be as simple as listing all the interactions and the potential data of interest in a table (or spreadsheet), something like this:

Activity/ Interaction	Object	Verb	Results	Context &/ or Extensions
User login/ logout, user views an object, takes a quiz, contributes to a discussion...	*Relevant object (a course object, url, form...)*	*Viewed, commented, attempted, commented, replied.....*	*Success, score, text...*	*Parent object, referring object, grouping, url*

We often find that it's easier to generate this list if we have an outline of our data goals, along with some wireframes or other relevant mockups. Then we do a walk-through of user interactions to make sure we are actually capturing all that we need to capture. Moreover, if we take a virtual journey through the course, it's easier to become aware of contextual information and how actions in the course interrelate.

After we have considered all the actions that are of value for our data needs, it's time to get a bit more specific. The table above can be used to create tables or spreadsheets documenting the vocabulary, so that we can compile the vocabulary we'll need for our xAPI statements. This will include verbs and activity types (and their respective IRIs) for each interaction. This is also a good place to enumerate design decisions that will impact data: details about things like how we will record time on site, or video views, or what counts as a completion.

This can take some time and thought, but it not only makes designing statements easier, it will make analysis easier down the road, because what seemed obvious when we designed a course in October might seem less clear when we are looking at the data in April. This brings us to the next reason why we want to make data stewardship a priority. . .

You'll Need to Teach Someone What You Did

You'll need to teach someone what you did, and that someone is probably you, six months from now.

It would be awesome if data analysis were always a well-planned, perfectly calm activity, but the real world produces other scenarios.

You're asked to pull some data about resource usage and performance in a course, and "Could you have some analysis and graphs to answer a set of, say, five questions ready by lunchtime?" And then the five questions turn into seven, and then eight, and "Can you also put in a quick written summary of the analysis?" Time is short, there's data to pull, then we need to check our data quality, check for outliers, do some analysis, give it a sense check, make some pretty graphs . . . and miraculously we get it done with three minutes to spare.

It's easy to think, "I'll remember how we set this analysis up" or "I'll make some quick notes on a Post-It and write it up later." Don't succumb to that temptation. You won't remember. The Post-It will get lost. And in a few months, or even weeks, you'll have no idea how you set up that clever analysis, or which criteria you used to determine outliers, or . . . Well, you get the idea.

Even if you never have to teach anyone how to do the analyses, even if no one ever asks you what criteria you used, or what decision you made, there's a good chance you'll be asked to do similar analyses or compare historical results, at some point down the road. So it's a good idea to document what you do, what criteria you use, and what issues you run into with data or data quality.

We have a lot of ways of doing this. We can create a text document or spreadsheet with a running list of actions, criteria, caveats. But we've also found, especially in the early stages that it's helpful to have a way to record that allows for the fact that approaches to analysis can evolve and iterate as we work with our data. One way to build a draft version of analysis documentation is very low-tech: a stack of notecards on a binder ring. Alternatively, we could have a second screen available to work on. The idea is to be able to see the process notes while doing the analysis. Putting the activities, in grueling detail, with each step or decision point on its own notecard or bullet point in a document, allows for detail to be captured and steps to be added, moved, or discarded as the process gets dialed in.

When we're developing the steps for an analysis, no detail is too trivial to document. Even notes to remember seemingly obvious fundamentals like, "do a sense check on the range of values," or specific notes about methods, like "outlier check via boxplot," should be recorded. It's then easy enough to flip through the deck, make sure the analysis can be replicated, and write it up formally for future reference. Real-world practice may mean that our data analyses are developed in somewhat chaotic circumstances, but we will thank ourselves if we put the process and the thoughts behind our decisions into a formal document that we can refer to in the future.

When Everybody's in Charge, Nobody's in Charge

As we've noted, despite our best efforts data projects often happen in the crucible of tight deadlines and capricious requests by our data customers. Plans can shift, with a lot of decisions made on the fly, regarding data collection or analysis, or how we've defined our verbs relative to the actual configuration of our course materials.

Even if we keep good documentation of our data collection and analysis practices, it's common for a number of people to have a hand in activities that will affect our data. The decisions of designers and developers come into play, as well as configuration of data sources outside of the control of the L&D department. What this all means is that there are many hands involved, and so we won't always know where our data comes from, or if changes were made that affect our analyses.

We don't necessarily need formal Data Governance protocols in place for our learning data, but we will need some planning and some communication to keep things on the rails. It's important to keep a list of who owns which data and which data processes, and to keep that list up to date. If we're pulling data from the CRM, we might not have control over when and how those data processes change, but we need to know that they have changed. If we have a Database Administrator running queries for us, we need not just confirmation that the query ran but documentation of the query itself, because, in the real world, it's possible to ask different DBAs for the same data and for different queries to result, if we are not informed (and accurate) enough about what we're asking for.

Managing data quality and consistency is a small, but critical, step that ensures that you get full value out of all the work you've done. Like all the other steps along the way, from strategic planning, to data collection, to analysis, it's not rocket science. If you perform each element with care, always keeping an eye on your goals and objectives, you will obtain valuable data, generate meaningful insights, and drive your projects forward to impact the performance of your learners and businesses.

References

Advanced Distributed Learning. "Experience XAPI Vocabulary Primer · Experience XAPI Vocabulary Primer." Adl (@adl) on GitBook · GitBook. Accessed January 26, 2017. https://adl.gitbooks.io/experience-xapi-vocabulary-primer/content/.

Advanced Distributed Learning. "Companion Specification for XAPI Vocabularies." Adl (@adl) on GitBook · GitBook. Accessed January 26, 2017. https://adl.gitbooks.io/companion-specification-for-xapi-vocabularies/content/.

Baum, David. "Data Quality, Data Governance, and Master Data Management (MDM)." Oracle | Integrated Cloud Applications and Platform Services. Accessed January 26, 2017. http://www.oracle.com/us/c-central/cio-solutions/information-matters/importance-of-data/index.html.

DuMoulin, Rob. "Where Data Governance Stops and Master Data Management Starts | Hub Designs Magazine." Hub Designs Magazine. Accessed January 26, 2017. https://hubdesignsmagazine.com/2011/10/13/where-data-governance-stops-and-master-data-management-starts/.

Howson, Cindi. *Successful Business Intelligence: Unlock the Value of BI & Big Data, Second Edition.* McGraw-Hill/Osborne, 2013.

Liebowitz, Jay. *Strategic Intelligence: Business Intelligence, Competitive Intelligence, and Knowledge Management.* Boca Raton: Auerbach Publications, 2006.

Loshin, David. "Data Governance for Master Data Management and Beyond." Analytics, Business Intelligence and Data Management | SAS. Accessed January 26, 2017. http://www.sas.com/content/dam/SAS/en_us/doc/whitepaper1/data-governance-for-MDM-and-beyond-105979.pdf.

Case Studies

Catholic Relief Services
By Brian Dusablon, Learning Ninjas

Catholic Relief Services (CRS) wanted to enhance a training program for staff involved in performing emergency needs assessments. At the time, they had an instructor-led course and a branching scenario they wanted to develop into an elearning module.

What started as a project to develop and improve a Storyline module turned into an opportunity to build a comprehensive xAPI blended program to learn more about how well the designed training prepared staff to perform a real assessment.

CRS mapped out the data with Rustici Software to develop a plan in Watershed LRS for reporting. A visual was created that showed the things that people needed to know and what tasks they needed to understand to perform well.

Below is an initial data point diagram we used to begin the discussions.

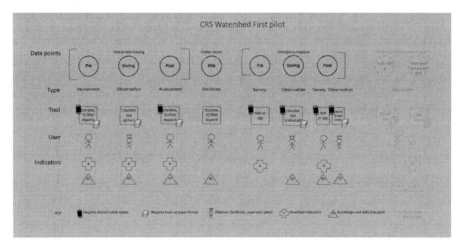

CRS and Learning Ninjas created a tool for instructors to create xAPI statements for a group of students in the classroom. The tool was an observation checklist that was uploaded to Watershed as a csv file. The statements for all the students in the class were uploaded as a group to see how they performed on the interview scenarios.

For the online learning portion of the program, we created a Storyline module that included a team selection interaction and a branching interview scenario. Storyline 1 was used "out of the box" for this project. We started designing the interview scenario with layers and a simple path, but quickly realized that Storyline would not generate statements from layers out of the box.

Upon learning how Storyline generates xAPI statements, we reconfigured the module to use slides, with detailed titles, so we were able to track the path a user took through the interactions. This made the course more complicated to manage because of the complex branching, but we were able to capture better data from our learners. We wanted to know what decisions learners were making in the team selection, including:

- How many times did it take them to put together the right team?
- What kind of team did they put together on the first try?
- Did they apply the guiding principles CRS uses in these field situations?

We also wanted to know where users were struggling in the interview scenario. Some of that data included:

- Were there any common failure points?
- Were the scenarios realistic?
- Were learners prepared enough to recover from an initial incorrect action? (For this module the scenario had three levels of failure from which they could recover.)

If 80% of users failed at a certain question, either the scenario was not accurate, or we needed to provide additional instruction for those types of interview situations. We were able to determine which areas we needed to investigate further to improve the scenario.

Finally, we designed an observation tool for CRS to capture live performance data for further comparison and analysis. CRS now has the capability to tie real-world performance in emergency response situations directly to their training scenarios. Not only does this help them determine if their training is effective, it also lets them utilize real world experiences to continuously improve their training.

The Ann Arbor Hands-On Museum
By Megan Torrance, TorranceLearning

The Big Picture

The Ann Arbor Hands-On Museum in Michigan provides a rich STEM-based informal learning experience for visitors with over 250 exhibits in 40,000 square feet of museum floor, along with classroom, outreach, and distance learning programs. Over 38,000 students in over 675 class field trip groups visit the museum every year.

All too often, the informal learning that takes place on a field trip doesn't transfer back to the classroom effectively. Students disperse upon arriving, their activity isn't recorded, and the connection with curriculum standards is increasingly difficult to establish. This makes it harder and harder for teachers to justify field trips when they're held to rigorous state-mandated academic standards.

The Digitally Enhanced Exhibit Program – DEEP – provides the engagement and collects the data to meet the dual needs of elementary educators and museum staff. Students on field trips interact with tablets placed at key exhibits. Using beacon name badges to automatically log students into the experience at each tablet, the appropriate grade level (or topic or language) experience is served on the screen. Third grade groups see third grade content, fifth graders interact with fifth grade content, and so on. The tablets guide the students through their interaction with the exhibit, offer challenges, ask questions, and spark reflection and application to new situations. All the while, the tablet records the experience, tracking the specific state science curriculum standards to which students are exposed on every screen, every exhibit tablet, by grade level.

At the end of the field trip, teachers receive detailed reports showing the curriculum standards that were experienced throughout the day. Visits and time spent on popular concepts and popular exhibits are reported before the teacher even gets back on the school bus. Free text and data entered by students at exhibits can be taken back to the classroom for use in other activities. Individual students each receive a personalized report showing the activities they experienced during the day along with their actual answers to questions and challenges posed at each of the exhibits they visited.

The museum has access to data about the length of time spent at each exhibit, the challenges completed, the data entered by students and the curriculum standards being exposed. Reports can display all data over all time, or calibrate to specific school or classroom-level reports.

Some More Details

DEEP is a truly novel combination of a number of emerging technologies that offers a simple and elegant solution to the challenge of creating a smart learning environment.
In the Hands-On Museum, students are assigned a name badge that includes a beacon with a unique identifier. Beacons are small, often inexpensive devices that enable more accurate location within a narrow range than GPS, cell tower triangulation and Wi-Fi proximity. Beacons transmit small amounts of data via Bluetooth Low Energy (BLE) up to 50 meters, and as a result are often used for indoor location technology, although beacons can be used outside as well. (Source: www.webopedia.com)

The DEEP beacon badges are arranged into classroom groups and assigned to a particular curriculum for the day. Currently the Museum offers 3rd, 4th and 5th grade curricula, with the ability to expand to additional grade levels, languages and related curricula (History of Science, Inventors & Inventions, Art & Design in Technology, etc.). The beacon badges identify the students as they approach DEEP-enabled exhibits so that the right curriculum can be served up to them and so their activities are tracked by the system.

Throughout the museum, DEEP-enabled exhibits have nearby iPad tablets mounted securely to the wall. Once a student has been identified at the museum, the tablet greets the student by badge name and the appropriate curriculum is automatically displayed on the screen. Visitors who don't have a DEEP badge can select a curriculum of their choosing from a START screen. The DEEP screens guide the children toward a more rich and informed interaction with the exhibit itself, posing challenges, asking questions, allowing for reflection and providing additional information. Text and graphics, multiple-choice and multiple-response, free text entry, drag-and-drop and other interactive techniques are used to engage students.

We identified very early on that this was an ideal situation for using the emerging xAPI specification for a number of reasons. While on its face this may look like just another fancy elearning application, the complexity and variety of interactions far exceeds the SCORM standard's capabilities. Whereas SCORM tracks a single logged-in LMS user at a time, DEEP handles multiple visitors in and out of the experience on a question-by-question level – and we certainly didn't want to slow down the children long enough to log in at each station!

DEEP takes advantage of xAPI to track what is otherwise a very informal learning experience at a level of detail that is ground-breaking. At each exhibit, each question is identified by the state science curriculum standards on a grade level basis. DEEP uses xAPI activity statements to record the student's responses, the correct answer (if one exists), the time spent per question, and, overall, who else was there at the time, the language used, and the curriculum standard by item number and description. All the data is stored in a LearnShare, LLC Learning Record Store (LRS) and available for reporting later on.

By using xAPI as the communication specification, DEEP is interoperable with other learning applications both now and into the future. This means that the system can be expanded, or the data gathered from a DEEP experience can be tracked and compared with other datasets. This interoperability and extensibility to future uses was a key factor in the museum's decision to pursue the project in this way.

At the end of the day, as a classroom turns in their DEEP badges and leaves the museum, staff print a set of reports that provide a rich picture of the students' visit. Teachers receive a report that shows the time spent and number of interactions with each exhibit and, perhaps more important, with each state curriculum standard. Frequently re-visited exhibits – the really popular ones with the kids – are highlighted as well. Students each receive a personalized report that shows details of their day at the museum, with an actual result from each of the DEEP exhibits they visited and the responses they entered. The museum will access more detailed ad hoc reporting allowing them to answer questions about the depth of the interactions, the time spent at exhibits, and the ways in which different classrooms use their time on their field trips. This rich data will allow the museum to make future improvements and recommendations.

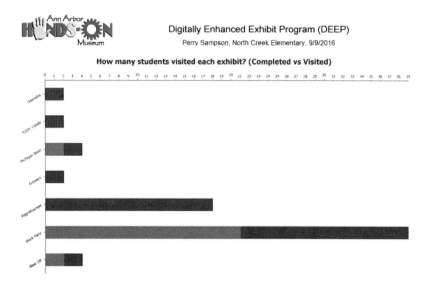

Which exhibits did students visit most frequently?

1. Block Party **22 total visits**, 0 total minutes spent
2. Magnetoscope **18 total visits**, 0 total minutes spent
3. Architect **2 total visits**, 0 total minutes spent
4. Michigan Basin **2 total visits**, 0 total minutes spent
5. H2Oh! Canals **2 total visits**, 0 total minutes spent
6. Geartable **2 total visits**, 0 total minutes spent

Appendix

Data Transfer

xAPI consists of multiple API resources: Statement, State, Agent, and Activity. In this section we will take a broad look at what each of these resources represents and how they work.

Statement API

The Statement API is the basic communication method of xAPI. When using the Statement API there are two methods to store a statement or statements in an LRS: the PUT method and the POST method. The PUT method stores a statement with a given ID. If the LRS already has a statement with the same ID, it will send an error code. The LRS cannot modify the ID of the incoming statement. The POST method stores a statement or a set of statements where an ID is not given. When using the POST method, the LRS cannot make any modifications to the state of a statement. So, if the state matches an existing statement, an error will be generated.

POST and form fields may use GET Statements to retrieve statements. GET Statements retrieve single or multiple statements. A list of statements is returned in a StatementResult Object. The object is a list of statements in reverse chronological order based on the time it was stored. The list generated is subject to permissions and a maximum list length. If there are more results than the object can handle, an IRI will be included for the additional results.

Document Resources

There are three APIs called the Document Resources which provide storage of data beyond statements. The data stored using the Document Resources give a view of the current situation at any point in time. Since the Document Resources look at the current state, instead of the past as in the Statement API, it is best not to use them for building reports of what has already happened (i.e. completions, pages visited, scores, etc.). Rather, if you're going to use the Document Resources to build a report, it would work well for real-time reporting since the data in the Document Resources can be constantly changing. For example, a completions report could be out of date very quickly. Document Resources could be used for a leaderboard. A leaderboard is constantly changing based on the learner activity, and real-time data is needed to run such a report. The Document Resources are made up of the State API, the Activity Profile API, and the Agent Profile API.

State API

The State API can be used by learning record providers as a method of bookmarking. The State API creates this data by storing the Activity and Agent as a pair. Simply put, the actor, or Agent, is paired together with the activity to provide feedback as to the location in a module of the learner. The State API can use four methods to PUT, POST, GET, or DELETE single documents by using the parameter stateID. The PUT and POST calls are used to write the statements to the LRS. These calls are specified in the code library that you are using to create the statements in the application. It simply specifies to the LRS what method will be used to write the statements. Depending on the LRS you are using, you might need to change the method in your code library for custom implementations. The GET call is used to retrieve statements. It would be used to retrieve the statements for visualization or for export purposes. It can also GET multiple documents by retrieving the available IDs and DELETE multiple documents through the context given other parameters. The DELETE function should be used by learning record providers to get rid of any documents that were stored for the purposes of preserving the state of the learning experience.

For example, when a screen in an eLearning module is left, but not completed by the learner, a state document might be stored so the learner to come back to that screen as they left it. Once the eLearning module is completed, that state document can be deleted.

Activity Profile API

The Activity Profile allows for arbitrary key/document pairs to be saved for a related activity, not related to a particular person. These documents would be stored across the activity. For example, if you are running a MOOC and you wanted to track the social interactions on comments between learners, the Activity Profile API can be used to store that data. It is driven by the profileID parameter. The profileID parameter specifies the profile that data will be drawn from or posted to along with the activityID. The Activity Profile API allows the full description of the activity to be retrieved from the LRS using the activityID parameter. The profileID parameter allows the PUT, POST, GET, and DELETE calls to be used for a single document. The GET call can be used with a timestamp to get all the entries that have been stored or updated since the specified timestamp. The GET call can also be used to get a definition of the activity from the LRS. There are many ways to setup the activity definition on the LRS. It can be built using information from statements stored in the LRS. Another method uses the Activity ID which contains a JSON file in the metadata that provides the definition of the activity. As well, the activity definition can come from somewhere outside the LRS. If given a choice, the best approach is to store the activity definition with the Activity ID.

Agent Profile API

The Agent Profile API also allows for arbitrary key/document pairs to be saved, but this time they are related to the Agent. The Agent Profile API allows for combined information on an agent to be collected from an outside service, such as a directory service (i.e. domain-controlled single sign-on). The profileID parameter is used for most single agent retrievals. The API allows for all profile entries of an agent to be collected. For example if an agent has multiple login criteria to a site, such as a company email and a Gmail account. The Agent Profile could be used to link those two accounts together to give the full profile of the agent.

Security

Security needs to be considered on all instances of an LRS and a learning record provider. In some cases the LRS provider will handle the LRS portion of the security. You will need to check with your IT provider that the transmission of statements is also secure.

The data collected has the potential to identify people and their training records. These records could be HR related, which should be protected and secured during run-time and for the storage of the statements. If you are deploying to mobile devices, it will add another level of complexity that needs to be accounted for in a project.

One of the great advantages of using xAPI is the ability to store statements without a connection to the LRS. If the delivery mechanism is able to store statements in an offline mode, the LRS can then accept the statements when communication is restored.

The xAPI specification addresses this and contains a section on security. In 2015, a document was authored called xAPIsec that addresses security recommendations to better support US Government security requirements. It recommends that all xAPI communication should be done through the Hypertext Transfer Protocol Secure (HTTPS) protocol, which provides the necessary security for the creation and movement of statements. There are also more specific recommendations:

- Use a strong signing algorithm such as SHA-256 to help determine data integrity.
- Use a strong key exchange such as Elliptic-Curve Diffie-Hellman which is an anonymous key agreement protocol.
- Leverage HTTP Strict Transport Security (HSTS) which sets the browser to maintain HTTPS once it has been set to help mitigate attacks.

Staying Up-to-Date

As xAPI advances, use these web resources for
the most up-to-date information:

- Connections Forum - http://connectionsforum.
  com runs events, workshops and offers training and
  publications related to xAPI and its best practices.
- The xAPI Quarterly - http://xapiquarterly.
  com/ is issues four times a year to offer a rich
  summary of the state of xAPI best practices.
- The Advanced Distributed Learning Initiative - http://
  adlnet.gov/ governs the xAPI specification and provides an
  index of its related official, authoritative documentation.
- The Data Interoperability Standards Consortium - http://
  datainteroperability.org/ bridges ADL's open source
  efforts by organizing community efforts that contribute
  to open efforts for data interoperability, like xAPI.

Acknowledgements

We would like to thank Aaron Silvers and Megan Bowe from MakingBetter for taking a chance on us and publishing this book. Without your never ending desire and drive to help us through this process this book would not have been possible. We are so grateful to you two for keeping us going and getting to this end result.

To all of our friends and colleagues for the discussions that helped us frame the direction that we took, we are forever in your debt. If there is ever anything we can do to help with your future projects, it would be an honor. Janet extends special thanks to her colleagues at HT2 Labs for their support and for always encouraging her to explore data more deeply.

To our editors, Megan Bowe and Catherine Skeen, thank you for helping us take the ideas in our heads and craft them into coherent messages on paper. Your countless hours of reading and editing our thoughts has made the final product into what it is today.

To Jason Early, the designer behind the cover and layout. Your artistic eye took a bunch of words and made it into something wonderful. Thank you.

Last, but certainly not least, a huge thank you to our families. Through the countless hours of writing, the writer's blocks that made us not so fun to be around, and the early failures that discouraged us, you were always behind us. We are forever grateful for your love and support.